Connecting the Dots
between life & faith

Rob *and* Lisa Laizure

Copyright © 2010 by Rob and Lisa Laizure

Connecting the Dots Between Life and Faith
by Rob and Lisa Laizure

Printed in China

ISBN 978-0-9819812-0-8

All rights reserved solely by the author. The author guarantees all contents are original and do not infringe upon the legal rights of any other person or work. No part of this book may be reproduced in any form without the permission of the author. The views expressed in this book are not necessarily those of the publisher.

Unless otherwise indicated, Bible quotations are taken from the New American Standard Bible. Copyright © 2006 by Thomas Nelson The MacArthur Study Bible.

The Holy Bible, New American Standard Version.
Used by permission.

www.dollarchristianbooks.com

TABLE OF CONTENTS

Connecting The Dots . . .

Chapter 1	Choices	7
Chapter 2	The Call From God	13
Chapter 3	When Trouble Comes	25
Chapter 4	Regarding Sin	41
Chapter 5	Family Problems	47
Chapter 6	Trails and Faith	55
Chapter 7	Regarding the Timing of God	69
Chapter 8	Set Apart for God	89
Chapter 9	Finally ...!	105
Chapter 10	Our Faith and How We Affect Others	113
Chapter 11	Surrendering It All	121
Chapter 12	The Simplicity of a Verse	133
References		145

CHAPTER 1

Choices

Life is filled with seasons. We are born, many of us go to school, get jobs, raise families, and eventually we die. However, in those years we have on this earth we make decisions each day. Some are small decisions and others are more difficult. Have you ever wondered why we make the decisions we do? What is our motivation to accept one job and reject another? What makes us want to go to one school in Chicago instead of California? What motivates us to go to a football game instead of baseball? Do we just decide things based on emotions? Do we make decisions based on how we were raised? What about decisions made based on religious beliefs?

All of our lives we have choices to make and many people base their choices on things like the world system, how they were raised, religious affiliation or the media. Many people feel they are born and it is up to them to make their way through life - as difficult as that may be. Many get tired and quit. Many succeed. What about those of us who claim to be Christians; those of us who are true followers of Jesus? Should we live life differently? Should we make different choices? What do we base those choices on?

For us, the first half of our lives were lived assuming God had dropped us here on earth and then left us alone to live however we thought best. We thought God was here on Sunday but Monday through Saturday we were on our own. We never recognized His hand in our lives on a day by day, moment by moment basis. We had to run our businesses and raise our children, and somehow, we separated our faith from our lives. It never really occurred to us that God wanted to be a part of our lives each day.

When we gave our hearts to Christ, we knew we had forgiveness of sins and assurance we would spend eternity in heaven, but what about the lives we lived every day? How did this faith affect the people we worked with, went to school with and our children? Did God really care if our business failed or succeeded? Did He really care where we sent our children to college? Was He that interested that we should actually talk with Him about these issues?

For most of our Christian life, we never knew what it meant to connect the dots between the faith we have in Jesus and what happened in our daily lives. We knew we were Christians, and yet somehow, accepting Him into our lives was all we thought we were supposed to do. As we grew in our faith, we realized that God wanted our faith and our lives to align. We began to realize that being a Christian did not just mean going to church each Sunday but it was supposed to be a way of life. We started seeing the hand of God in things that we were accustomed to controlling, like business deals and what decisions our children were making.

My (Rob) first encounter with connecting my life and faith was with a business deal many years ago. We were in the Outdoor Advertising Business and I was a new believer. I had always made the decisions for our company and because I had always been in charge of that, asking God for help and guidance was a different thought process for me. I was in business with a Christian friend of mine and we had both run out of money. The business we acquired had to be given back to the original owner who happened to be a very tough business man. Since we knew the type of person he was, we went to the meeting to give his business back to him knowing there was no way he would ever help us. What happened was completely shocking. This man, who was not known for his kindness, decided to let us continue on in the business and allowed us to pay him interest only for three years to help us get our company going. Automatically this helped cash flow, our business, and it gave us our start in the Outdoor Advertising Business. For me, it was the first time in my life I connected the dots between my life (my business) and my faith. Suddenly, I realized it was God in control of this deal and not me. I always thought I had to make things happen and yet I recognized God's hand in this, knowing He alone was the only One who could and did change this man's heart to help us.

Proverbs 21:1, "The king's heart is like channels of water in the hand of the Lord; He turns it wherever He wishes."

This was my first encounter with God taking a person's heart and changing it. I began to see how God works. I am called to be diligent and put all the effort into our business plans and ideas; yet ultimately it is God who is guiding our lives and our businesses. When I figured this out, my life took a more peaceful turn because as I prayed, I knew God was the One who would help us be successful or not. If we succeeded – He would get all the credit. If we didn't succeed, we would know He was moving us to a different place in our lives.

Deuteronomy 8:18, "But you shall remember the Lord your God, for it is He who is giving you power to make wealth, that He may confirm His covenant which He swore to your fathers, as it is this day."

For me (Lisa), my first encounter with connecting the dots between my faith and real life was with one of our sons. This incident happened right after the 9/11 tragedy and for some reason he and his friends thought it would be funny to take a back pack and leave it by a garbage can at a movie theatre and see the reaction of people. Not such a bright idea since security was heightened because of what had just occurred in New York. As he was putting the back pack there, he and his friends started running away just as an undercover policeman walked outside and saw them do this. Needless to say, in a few minutes our son was in handcuffs on the ground. Since he was eighteen at the time he could have gone to jail, but instead, the police called our house. What was interesting was we had just bought a new phone that day and when the call came in Rob was on the phone and didn't know how to switch the call over, so our son was released into the custody of the other boy's father.

When we did get the call from our friend, explaining what happened and how he had the boys with him, we were furious. Then it hit me. God is in control. If God is in control of our son's life then what is it that He wants to teach him? At the time he was a drummer in a Christian band and maybe He wanted our son to start connecting the dots between his life and his faith. A few things went through my mind. If Rob had gotten the call from the police he probably would have told them to take our son to jail to teach him a lesson- I was thankful for buying a new phone that day. Instead of going crazy and screaming and yelling we had this sense of calm that God was in control trying to teach our son something about his life. Suddenly, instead of taking matters into our own hands, we really gave the situation over to God. He did get in trouble, but instead of being upset and worrying we realized God was in this situation, as He is in all our situations. All we could do was pray that God would teach our son what he needed to know.

Therein lies the peace of God. What do we do when bad things happen? How do we react when we lose a job, don't make the football team or don't get into the college we applied for? What happens when our children make poor choices? What do we do when tragedy strikes us? How do we recognize the hand of God in our lives?

As Christians, the Bible makes it clear in **Psalm 46:10 "Be still, and know that I am God; I will be exalted among the**

nations, I will be exalted in the earth!", we need to learn to be still and to wait on God knowing all along He has a purpose and plan behind all He allows into our lives. Many times God will use difficult times to get us to where He wants us to be. Nothing is ever out of His control.

Abraham, in the Old Testament, is a great example of someone learning how to connect the dots between his life and his faith. Abraham was raised in a non-Christian home where his father worshipped false gods. The One True God called Abraham and promised to make him a great nation, which we know today as the Jewish nation. All through his life he had to learn how to trust God, and yet, as we will see, even Abraham made many mistakes.

That is why the Bible is so great because it uses great men of the Bible with all their faults and flaws to teach us how to live our lives today. Abraham had to learn, just like us, that God wants to be a part of our daily lives. He wants to teach us how to connect the dots between our beliefs in Christ and how that plays out on a daily basis in our lives. Please join us on this journey into Abraham's life as he learned how to trust God in difficult situations, how to deal with forgiveness, how to deal with family struggles and yet through it all trust God above all else. Through the life of Abraham, our hope and prayer is that we will learn how to integrate our faith with our real lives.

Dots to Connect

- Our relationship with God must influence the choices we make in life.

- God is the One who changes other peoples' hearts to get us where He wants us.

- Being a Christian is not just about church on Sunday – it is a day to day experience that infiltrates every part of our life.

- All events in our lives must be a part of connecting the dots between our faith and God's will for us.

Chapter 2

The Call From God

Did you ever realize that God speaks to us? Very rarely does He speak audibly but instead He uses the Bible, a sermon at church, a bible study, our daily circumstances or the Holy Spirit's prompting in our hearts. In the days before the Bible came into being, God spoke directly to a few people. He used things like visions and dreams and mainly spoke through prophets, but God spoke directly to Abraham. We read this in **Genesis 12:1-3, "Now the Lord said to Abram, 'Go forth from your country, and from your relatives and from your father's house, to the land which I will show you; and I will make you a great nation, and I will bless you, and make your name great; and so you shall be a blessing; and I will bless those who bless you, and the one who curses you I will curse. And in you all the families of the earth will be blessed.'"** Abraham had a choice; to listen to God or ignore Him. Thankfully, Abraham did exactly what God called him to do.

Genesis 12:4, "So Abram went forth as the Lord had spoken to him; and Lot went with him. Now Abram was seventy-five years old when he departed from Haran."

The first dot we want to connect is that if you are a Christian today it is because God has called you. **John 6:44** says, **"No one can come to Me unless the Father who sent Me draws him; and**

I will raise him up on the last day." John 6:65 says, "And He was saying, "For this reason I have said to you, that no one can come to Me unless it has been granted him from the Father." Our salvation is a direct result of God calling us to Himself and just like Abraham, He has a purpose for our lives. Somehow we do not connect the two: our life and God's purpose for us. Somehow we think our birth was just a random thing that happened in the universe and yet the God who created us is the One who orchestrated the entire event!

Acts 17:25-27 says, "nor is He served by human hands, as though He needed anything, since He Himself gives to all people life and breath and all things; and He made from one man every nation of mankind to live on all the face of the earth, having determined their appointed times and the boundaries of their habitation, that they would seek God, if perhaps they might grope for Him and find Him, though He is not far from each one of us."

We need to recognize HE is the one who gives us life and breath and HE has determined our boundaries in life. When we read verses like these it makes us realize, maybe for the first time, that God has a plan for us. Our life is not an accident and our salvation is not an accident. We are placed here to serve God and be used by Him to share Him with others and help others grow in their faith.

There is something exciting about being able to connect this dot, for in it, our lives have purpose and meaning. So many people go through their days wondering why they are here and wondering what the reason is for living. When we can connect God to our lives in such a personal way, everything takes on a new meaning. Here are two places we must learn to connect the dots; our workplace and our homes.

Our Work • • •

When we connect this dot, our workplace will take on new

meaning. When we realize it was God who gave us our talent to be a doctor, lawyer, teacher or salesperson, we can then use our job where God has placed us to be witnesses for Him. **Colossians 3:23** says, **"Whatever you do, do your work heartily, as for the Lord rather than for men."** When we realize He is a part of all we do, we will become men and women of integrity and honesty in our work places. We will love and care for others more than ourselves because we know that God is working in every detail of our lives.

Philippians 2:13 says, **"for it is God who is at work in you, both to will and to work for His good pleasure."**

The people around us should be able to see a difference in us. How do we respond to our boss? How do we treat our customers or the person in the next office? Do our lives reflect the belief we have in Jesus? We heard of a woman who was asked what she did for a living and her response was, "I am a fully devoted follower of Jesus Christ cleverly disguised as an airline stewardess." What a great response, which begs the question; is that how we view our job? Do we say we are fully devoted followers of Jesus cleverly disguised as a dentist or nurse or police officer? Does our devotion to Christ precede our job and if so, is that affecting our work place? What is our speech like at work? How do we handle difficult situations? Do we love those who are difficult to love and work with? Do our lives reflect Christ so when we invite someone to church with us they don't think we are hypocrites?

When we can connect this dot, our work place becomes a mission field. We begin to recognize that we are either helping others come to Christ or we are turning them away.

2 Corinthians 2:14-16 says, **"But thanks be to God, who always leads us in triumph in Christ, and manifests through us the sweet aroma of the knowledge of Him in every place. For we are a fragrance of Christ to God among those who are being saved and among those who are perishing; to the one an aroma from death**

to death, to the other an aroma from life to life. And who is adequate for these things?"

Are we bringing the fragrance of Christ to our workplace?

Our Home Life . . .

Our homes will be different when we know God has a purpose and plan for our families. The problem is the lack of knowledge regarding what that purpose is. Today we were at a class at church and we were talking to a newly married young couple. Because they had not studied their Bible enough to know their roles, they were confused. Someone had told the wife that she was to always do what her husband wanted because he was always right. It made us realize how messed up marriages can become when there is a lack of truth. This cute couple had so many questions and the majority of the questions were based on something they had been told which was rooted in half truths.

What someone told her was most likely rooted in **Ephesians 5:22, "Wives, submit to your husbands as to the Lord"**. In her mind, submitting to her husband meant she had to be a door mat where he could walk over her. To her it probably meant she could never speak her mind and she had to go along with her husband regardless of how she felt. Nothing could be further from the truth. We tried to explain to her that a marriage is not based on one verse but, in this case, a group of verses. God has a great plan for how marriages are to work and it involves both husbands and wives. For men, here is their role:

Ephesians 5:25, "Husbands, love your wives, just as Christ also loved the church and gave Himself up for her", and adds in **Colossians 3:19, "Husbands, love your wives and do not be embittered against them"**.

God calls men to love their wives like Christ loved the

Church which means since He died for the church and gave everything up for her, husbands are to do the same for their wives. The implications to this are enormous. Men have to love their wives more than their own lives. The Bible talks about love in 1 Corinthians 13 and in order for a man to love his wife, he must love his wife with these attributes. The Message paraphrases love in this way:

1 Corinthians 13:4-7, "Love never gives up. Love cares more for others than for self. Love doesn't want what it doesn't have. Love doesn't strut, doesn't have a swelled head, doesn't force itself on others, isn't always 'me first', doesn't fly off the handle, doesn't keep score of the sins of others, doesn't revel when others grovel, takes pleasure in the flowering of truth, puts up with anything, trusts God always, always looks for the best, never looks back, but keeps going to the end." (The Message Version)

I (Rob) always say we men got the worst end of this deal! We are the ones who are responsible for being patient and kind to our wives; we have to care more for them and their feelings than ourselves. We can't be easily angered and we can't keep a record of what our wives do wrong. Basically, we are called to treat our spouse with the kind of love that Jesus showed us, meaning He gave up everything. Our pride, rudeness and arrogance have to go and must be replaced with humility and caring about our wife's needs more than our own. Our job is virtually impossible and without the help of the Holy Spirit living in us and changing us, it cannot happen.

We have four boys who are now married and the dot I want them to connect is this: "happy wife, happy life." I spent the first ten years of my marriage not understanding that my life had to be about Lisa and what was best for her. I had to learn I wasn't there to be her Holy Spirit and tell her what to do all the time. I wasn't married so I could rule over her and make her submit to my wishes and desires. My part was to love her and pray for her. I was to trust God to change her heart on the things that needed to be changed. The dot I needed to connect was that I was to be more concerned for what God calls

me to do not about what He calls **her** to do. My job was to make sure I was reading my Bible and learning how to be a godly man and discover how to care more for the things of God than the things of Rob and as I learn that, my marriage thrives.

As we were talking with this couple, our pastor walked up and they asked if the church had marriage counseling. He said they did but his suggestion was to go through the class that teaches people how to grow in their lives spiritually. He basically explained that without knowing biblically how to be transformed from the inside, it wouldn't matter what they were taught in a marriage class. God is the only one who can produce in us the ability to have successful marriages.

Women on the other hand are called to do two things: submit and respect. Both of these are tremendously easy when your husband is doing what he is called to do. For me (Lisa), submitting is simple because I have a husband who loves me. He never tells me what to do or demands I do what he says but instead, he is a servant-leader. He leads me by serving me and therefore he is easy to follow. Submitting does not mean I am a door mat and he walks all over me. Instead, we are a team and on each team for it to work there has to be a leader and a follower.

Because Rob loves me and cares more for me than himself, then he listens to me. If we have a decision to make, he always asks my thoughts and opinions. He takes everything into consideration before he makes a final decision, including me in what he is thinking. When he does make a decision, I know it will be a good one because he is trusting God. He prays about the choices he has to make and therefore I can be confident when he does make a decision because I trust God is speaking to him.

Respect is the other part of what we women are called to do. **Ephesians 5:33** says to wives, "**Nevertheless, each individual among you also is to love his own wife even as himself, and the**

wife must see to it that she respects her husband." Synonyms for the word respect are things like: admiration, high opinion, reverence, value and esteem. When we have respect for our husbands it means we hold them in high regard, we appreciate them, and we admire them. It is easy to respect and admire a man that treats us well and it seems if the man is doing his part, loving his wife, and the wife is doing their part, submitting and respecting; the marriage should be a wonderful institution.

This is God's plan for marriage. When men and women refuse to play out their roles it can have devastating effects. When a man is uncaring, unthoughtful, selfish and angry – it is difficult for a woman to submit and respect him. Abraham will learn this in a very valuable way through his life. He learns very quickly how selfishness on his part can be very destructive to his marriage.

Marriages are falling apart and the worst part is that this is happening to those who claim to be followers of Christ. When we get married, there is no more second guessing if we married the right person or not. We did. We have to recognize God's hand in our married life. Could God have stopped us from marrying the person we did? Absolutely! However, since He didn't, then that is the person He has for us. Once we settle that in our heart and our minds then we can start learning how to love that person as God has called us to. Love is not a feeling as much as it is a commitment and we must be able to look at our marriages as the place where He has called us.

Deuteronomy 6:6-7, "These words, which I am commanding you today, shall be on your heart. You shall teach them diligently to your sons and shall talk of them when you sit in your house and when you walk by the way and when you lie down and when you rise up."

We have to teach our children how to connect the dots in marriage. We would like to leave our children a legacy of what a godly marriage looks like. Do we model this all the time? Are we always loving, kind and selfless? No way. But when we fail, we talk about it to our children. We apologize to them; we talk to them about why we acted the way we did. We keep our lines of communication open so they can see what a marriage looks like and when we do have issues we can teach them how to fix them in a biblical manner. If we can model how to live together as God intended, then our children will be able to follow in our footsteps.

Teaching children about God has to be a daily occurrence. As things come up during the day, God has to be attached to each situation. If our youngest daughter starts talking about boys, it gives us a great opportunity to talk with her about the qualities she should look for in order to have a great marriage. If our youngest son watches a movie and is disturbed by something he sees we are able to explain why he should be upset and how the world looks at life differently than we as Christians do. Everything is a life lesson for them pointing them to the abundant life that Jesus has promised us.

God is a very personal God. He cares about our work, our homes and how we treat others. He cares about our children and grandchildren, where we go to school and where we get a job. He cares about the smallest details of our lives.

Many years ago Rob and I were looking to buy some property in Montana. There was something about the scenery, the rivers and the blue skies that captured our hearts. We found some land and put a contract on it but as the days wore on I started feeling very uncomfortable about buying this property. Rob was still convinced we should purchase it and since we both disagreed I started praying. If we were not to have the land, God would have to change Rob's heart, which He didn't seem to be doing. The day before we had to close on the land, Rob was in the office which was on the other side of the wall from our bedroom. I was praying on one side of the wall and Rob was doing his devotions on the other side. When he was finished, he came around the corner and told me he felt like God was impressing on his heart not to buy the property. For me, it was one of those moments where I saw in action how God clearly changed his heart. It was then I realized how much God really does care about even the little things in our lives.

He did not put us on earth and leave us to fend for ourselves; instead, He wants to be a part of all we do. Once we recognize His hand in our lives, then we can have peace and assurance in the troubled times. He is even in control over the tough times in our lives and if we can learn to trust Him through the difficulties, we come out on the other end knowing He has purposes beyond what we could imagine.

Ephesians 3:20, "Now to Him who is able to do far more abundantly beyond all that we ask or think, according to the power that works within us."

God Moves us where He Wants Us! • • •

Abraham heard the call of God and obeyed. He trusted Him enough to pull up stakes and move with his family to a foreign land. Just like Abraham, we need to learn to listen for the voice of God and then do what He commands. He is an incredible God who moves on the hearts of His people to move them where He wants. If you apply for a certain job and do not get it – you can be assured God turned the hearts of the employer because He wants you somewhere else. If your boyfriend or girlfriend breaks up with you, be assured God has moved on a heart for this to happen. He has a perfect plan for your life and most times we cannot see it and yet we can live with peace and comfort knowing He moves people where He wants them.

Just like Abraham, God called him and moved on his heart to leave the only home he knew for a distant land. When God calls us places, He will move our hearts to where He wants us to go. Many people are afraid God will call them to a distant land to be missionaries and yet we know God would move on the hearts of the people to want to go. We had missionaries leave from our church to go to Turkey to share Christ with the Muslim people. These two had recently been married and just had a baby and yet nothing would change their minds regarding the mission field. Why? Because God moved their hearts and when He does that, just like Abraham, we go. Not everyone is called to a foreign country; most are just called to our neighborhoods and workplaces. We have a mission field right where we live so unless God has moved your heart someplace else – relax! Be used by Him right where you are.

There are family members, co-workers, neighbors and friends who need Jesus and most times He leaves us right where we are in order to serve Him. The point to Abraham is that when God called him, he listened and went because God had an incredible plan for his life. The entire Jewish nation began with one man – Abraham. The roots of Jesus go back to this man – Abraham. The land of Israel was promised to the descendants of one man – Abraham. All because he heard the call and allowed God to transform his life and his way of thinking. Once we start connecting the dots of our faith and life, we too, like Abraham, can recognize His call on our lives. We too can be used of Him because He has a plan for our lives just as He had a plan for Abraham's.

2 Timothy 1:8-9, "Therefore do not be ashamed of the testimony of our Lord or of me His prisoner, but join with me in suffering for the gospel according to the power of God, who has saved us and called us with a holy calling, not according to our works, but according to His own purpose and grace which was granted us in Christ Jesus from all eternity."

Philippians 2:13, "For it is God who is at work in you, both to will and to work for His good pleasure."

Ephesians 2:10, "For we are His workmanship, created in Christ Jesus for good works, which God prepared beforehand so that we would walk in them."

Dots to Connect

- If you are a Christian, it is because God has called you into a relationship with Him.

- God has placed you in the job, the neighborhood, or the school that you are in so you can be used by Him to win others to Jesus.

- God has a purpose and a plan for your life.

- Our home and work are two places where God should be at the center.

- God cares about even the smallest details in our lives.

- God moves our hearts to go where He wants us to go.

Chapter 3

When Trouble Comes

The next dot we want to connect is the fact we are not immune to trouble in our lives. Many people, when they come to Christ, assume their lives will be smooth sailing from there on and yet the Bible never says that is true. Abraham finds this out soon enough! He has now left his home and family for a distant land, listening to the voice of God and no sooner does he get to the land God wants him and there is a problem – a famine and wicked people. Suddenly, this place that Abraham thought he would settle down in and live happily ever after, he realized, had a few problems. When unexpected things come into our lives – what do we do? Do we panic? Do we worry? Do we take matters into our own hands?

Somehow we do not seem to associate trouble...with God. We think He only wants us to be happy, healthy and wealthy at all times so when trouble comes our way we somehow think God has skipped out on us. We need to recognize that is never true. **Isaiah 45:6-7** says, **"That men may know from the rising to the setting of the sun that there is no one besides Me. I am the Lord, and there is no other, the One forming light and creating darkness, causing well-being and creating calamity; I am the Lord who does all these."** The questions always arise with one word: WHY? Why would God create calamity? Why would He allow bad things to happen in our lives? Why would He allow tragedy, loss of job or loss of life to enter into our lives? Many times it is because God wants to move us to different places. Most of the time we might never know, so we will have to claim this verse, **Isaiah 55:8-9, "For My thoughts are not your thoughts, nor are your ways My ways,"** declares the Lord. **"For as the heavens are higher than the earth, so are My ways higher than your ways And My thoughts than your thoughts."** We have to start recognizing God for who He is. He is in control. His ways are higher than our ways. Many times we will have to learn to trust His ways without ever having the "why" question answered.

Abraham is now in the land God had called him to and then a famine strikes. Suddenly, there is no food for his family and this is what happens, **Genesis 12:10, "Now there was a famine in the land; so Abram went down to Egypt to sojourn there, for the famine was severe in the land."** The problem with this verse is it doesn't tell us what we want to know. Did Abraham consult God regarding his fear of no food? Did Abraham ask God to provide for him? Did Abraham become anxious and leave for Egypt on his own? Was everyone around him going to Egypt so he just assumed that was what he was supposed to do also?

We never know why Abraham leaves but his actions in the next verse shows us he was living in fear; fear for his own life. When we replace trust for fear – things always turn out badly.

Genesis 12:11-13, "It came about when he came near to Egypt, that he said to Sarai his wife, 'See now, I know that you are a beautiful woman; and when the Egyptians see you, they will say, This is his wife; and they will kill me, but they will let you live. Please say that you are my sister so that it may go well with me because of you, and that I may live on account of you.'"

Here it shows us that even the great men of the bible had lapses in judgement. They became fearful; they stopped trusting in God and focused on their own personal well being. When we start doing that – we usually end up in trouble!

Abraham's wife, Sarai, was a very beautiful woman and instead of trusting his life to God, Abraham decided to take matters in his own hands. He wanted her to lie for him – he wanted her to tell the Egyptians she was his sister! That way, when Pharaoh wanted her to be part of his harem – they wouldn't kill Abraham – they would take his wife and let him live. What happened to his wedding vows? What happened to his job of being his wife's protector? What happened to Abraham trusting God?

Trusting God in tough situations is the most difficult part of life. We lack patience. We need answers now. We can't see what God is doing so we feel panic. As we are writing this the economy is the worst it has been since we can remember. People are losing jobs and homes and businesses are going under on each corner. For us, we are learning to trust God daily for His provisions for our business but in all truthfulness, it is much easier to trust ourselves to work hard than to trust God to provide. Why is that? Maybe it is because we cannot see Him. Maybe because we cannot pick up the phone and call Him. Maybe in the back of our minds we can't imagine that He truly cares about how many crowns we receive each day at our dental lab.

A few weeks ago we were not sure what to do with our dental crown business. Because of the economy, people are not getting the dental work done they need because of the expense. All of our boys work for this company and our usual crown count at that time was 40-45 per day. Suddenly, in one week the count went down to 18-25 which is a huge drop that we weren't sure our company could withstand. So we prayed. We prayed for God to show us what to do. Do we walk away from this company? Do we stop investing money in it? What happens to our children who work there? So many questions and God seemed silent, up to that point.

That afternoon we got the crown count for the day which was a record 76! It was one of those moments where God wanted to remind us that He had not forgotten about us. Keep going, keep persevering and keep working hard. Thomas Edison was a famous inventor in the late 1800's and early 1900's who said, *"Many of life's failures are people who did not realize how close they were to success when they gave up."* God calls us to work hard. He would make sure our business would succeed if that was His plan for us. He would provide the money needed to sustain it. The problem is we want to know how. How will You provide for us? We have property that needs to be sold, but in this economy that seems impossible. We have money in an account that has been shut down for months that we cannot get to. How God? How will You make this happen? That is where trust comes in – we don't know how, but we trust He will.

"Even if..."

Another dot we need to connect between our life and faith is learning that God does not always do what we want. When we give our lives, our businesses, our jobs, our children and our families to Him, sometimes He has different plans for us than we do. What we need to recognize is the fact that God is in charge of the outcome and we have to learn to trust Him **"even if"** He doesn't come through the way we would like. When we love God and recognize His hand in everything we do then life has a peaceful existence about it because even though we do not always get what we want; we know we get His best for us. A perfect example of this in the Bible is the story of Daniel's friends Shadrach, Meshach and Abed-nego.

In 605 B.C. the Babylonians conquered Jerusalem and Daniel and his three friends were exiled to Babylon, a foreign country with foreign gods. As the years went by, Nebuchadnezzar, King of Babylon decided to build a golden image and expected the people to bow down and worship it.

Daniel 3:4-8, Then the herald loudly proclaimed: "To you the command is given, O peoples, nations and men of every lan-

guage, that at the moment you hear the sound of the horn, flute, lyre, trigon, psaltery, bagpipe and all kinds of music, you are to fall down and worship the golden image that Nebuchadnezzar the king has set up. But whoever does not fall down and worship shall immediately be cast into the midst of a furnace of blazing fire. Therefore at that time, when all the peoples heard the sound of the horn, flute, lyre, trigon, psaltery, bagpipe and all kinds of music, all the peoples, nations and men of every language fell down and worshiped the golden image that Nebuchadnezzar the king had set up. For this reason at that time certain Chaldeans came forward and brought charges against the Jews."

The problem for Shadrach, Meshach and Abed-nego is that they were Jewish men who followed God and worshipping a false god or idol was something they would never do.

Daniel 3:12-15, "There are certain Jews whom you have appointed over the administration of the province of Babylon, namely Shadrach, Meshach and Abed-nego. These men, O king, have disregarded you; they do not serve your gods or worship the golden image which you have set up. Then Nebuchadnezzar in rage and anger gave orders to bring Shadrach, Meshach and Abed-nego; then these men were brought before the king. Nebuchadnezzar responded and said to them, Is it true, Shadrach, Meshach and Abed-nego, that you do not serve my gods or worship the golden image that I have set up? Now if you are ready, at the moment you hear the sound of the horn, flute, lyre, trigon, psaltery and bagpipe and all kinds of music, to fall down and worship the image that I have made, very well. But if you do not worship, you will immediately be cast into the midst of a furnace of blazing fire; and what god is there who can deliver you out of my hands?"

These three men had a serious problem. They were being asked to bow down and worship a false image and yet their faith in God would not allow for that to happen. They loved God more than they loved their lives and faced with this situation, they refused to compromise. Their response to the king was this:

Daniel 3:17-18 "If it be so, our God whom we serve is able to deliver us from the furnace of blazing fire; and He will deliver us out of your hand, O king. But even if He does not, let it be known to you, O king, that we are not going to serve your gods or worship the golden image that you have set up."

This response is the same response we need to have in any given situation and is worth repeating, **"But even if He does not, let it be known to you, O king, that we are not going to serve your gods or worship the golden image that you have set up."**

Our faith cannot rise or fall based upon what God does or does not do for us. Our faith has to stand strong and steady even in the midst of turmoil and trials. For these three men, they trusted in the fact that God could save them at any moment and yet they knew God might have a different plan which could mean their death. For us it could be situations like these:

God could get me the job I want, *but if He doesn't...*
God could save my marriage, *but if He doesn't...*
God could heal my sickness, *but if He doesn't...*
God could allow me to have the child I have always wanted, *but if He doesn't...*
God could provide clients for our business, *but if He doesn't...*
God could sell our home, *but if He doesn't...*
God could make sure the person I am dating will marry me, *but if He doesn't...*
God could save my drug addicted child from a life of heartache, *but if He doesn't...*
God could have allowed my loved one to live, *but since He didn't...*
God could have stopped my spouse from having an affair, *but since He didn't...*
God could have saved my family member before he died,

but since He didn't...

We have to learn to say:

> I will never walk away from my faith,
> I will always trust You,
> I will always love You.

The connection between our life and faith is so important to our every day! All through our lives we will have problems and trials and yet just like Daniel's three friends, they KNEW God could do anything. They also knew if God didn't do what they wanted, which consisted of saving their lives, then it was okay. Their faith in Him did not depend on if or how He answered their prayers. We have to be resolute in our faith, refusing to waver when things do not go our way. We have to relax and know that He is God when our world seems to be falling apart. We need to realize that most of the time we cannot see what He is doing, from His vantage point, but He wants us to trust Him anyway.

We have a daughter who struggles with faith. She struggles with believing there is a God, she questions how He could have created this world and how He could save our sins. But through it all she has determined not to let her faith waver. "Even if" she never has enough faith to truly feel what she believes – she will believe anyway. "Even if" she doesn't feel the presence of God, she will trust He is there. "Even if" she never hears His voice, she will read His Word and trust what it says. She has learned her faith is not dependent on her feelings. Just like Daniel's friends who trusted God could save them, but might not, we too need to learn to be "even if" kind of people.

Remembering Stones • • •

One day, Rob was having an exceptionally difficult day at

work and everything that was happening made him feel defeated. Rob is the one in the family who is always the positive, "glass half full" guy so when he gets down we never know what to say. That night I was telling our youngest son, Dusty, about remembering stones.

Joshua 4:21-24, He said to the sons of Israel, "When your children ask their fathers in time to come, saying, 'What are these stones?' then you shall inform your children, saying, 'Israel crossed this Jordan on dry ground.' For the Lord your God dried up the waters of the Jordan before you until you had crossed, just as the Lord your God had done to the Red Sea, which He dried up before us until we had crossed; that all the peoples of the earth may know that the hand of the Lord is mighty, so that you may fear the Lord your God forever."

It dawned on me that we needed to give Rob some "remembering stones" so he could remember how God has brought us through in the past. Dusty sat down and drew out a picture of stones stacked on one another and we started writing down things, in the past, God had done for us. He sold our house the exact day we had written a contract on another home. He turned the heart of a tough businessman so we could stay in the advertising business. He brought a buyer for a spec home we had built. He sold our outdoor business at the last minute possible. He changed the heart of our son and an old girlfriend to bring them back together. He did all these things and He waited until the last minute so we could never say we did any of it. It was all Him.

We need remembering stones in our lives so when times become desperate, we can remember that God really does come through. Someone once said, "He is always late but always on time." This is so true! We always think He is late in His answers and yet how would we ever learn to trust Him if He always answered the day we prayed for something? God would be our "genie in the bottle" instead of the God who loves and cares for us and wants us to learn how to depend on Him.

Now back to Abraham. **Genesis 12:14-16** goes on to tell us, **"It came about when Abram came into Egypt, the Egyptians saw that the woman was very beautiful. Pharoah's officials saw her and praised her to Pharoah; and the woman was taken into Pharoah's house. Therefore he treated Abram well for her sake; and gave him sheep and oxen and donkeys and male and female servants and female donkeys and camels."** Sounds like life was working for Abraham but Sarai was in serious trouble. Pharoah thought she was beautiful and she ended up in his harem. Somehow Abraham must have thought he was helping God out and yet this would be a great lesson that God doesn't really need our help!

Because Pharoah liked Sarai, he gave Abraham gifts – many animals and male and female servants. The lesson Abraham would learn, from his distrust in God, would be detrimental to our world...even to this day. The wars between Israel and the Palestinian nation 4,000 years later are a direct result of what Abraham did with one of his servants from Egypt. What Abraham will learn is there are always serious consequences to not obeying and trusting God. The Bible says in **Galatians 6:7 "Do not be deceived, God is not mocked; for whatever a man sows, this he will also reap."** Abraham is about to learn is that he cannot thwart God's plan. If Abraham would not protect Sarai – God would. Here is what God did in order to get Sarai out of the trouble her husband caused her.

Genesis 12:17-20, "But the Lord struck Pharoah and his house with great plagues because of Sarai, Abram's wife. Then Pharoah called Abram and said, 'What is this you have done to me? Why did you not tell me that she was your wife? Why did you say, She is my sister, so that I took her for my wife? Now then, here is your wife, take her and go.' Pharoah commanded his men concerning him; and they escorted him away, with his wife and all that belonged to him."

God came through and saved Sarai but this whole situation had to be embarrassing to Abraham. Here he was, a man of God, the Bible calls him a man of faith and now he would return to the land God promised him slightly embarrassed. Once Pharoah realized the great plagues were a direct result of Abraham's lie – he escorted him out of town.

Abraham's problem is what most of us struggle with: selfishness. We have to constantly be checking our heart to see if we are caring more for others or for ourselves. Abraham was thinking of himself and because of this, there were serious consequences to his actions. Just like Abraham, a man of faith, it took years of learning lessons just like it does for us.

When we hurt someone we must learn to apologize. Many people say they are sorry but there are no changes in their actions. Our youngest son has a habit of this. He does something wrong, gets in trouble, apologizes and then does the same thing again. We finally told him that apologies don't mean anything if there is no change in behavior. When we recognize a destructive behavior in our lives like jealousy, possessiveness, anger, fear, or selfishness, we must recognize it and pray desperately for the Holy Spirit to work to change us from the inside. Apologies are worthless if it doesn't move us to a behavioral change. As we grow in our faith and grow closer to Christ, the bible says in **John 3:30 "He must increase, but I must decrease."** Our actions need to be more about God and others than ourselves. This was a difficult lesson for Abraham to learn.

Here are a couple points to learn from this story:
- If we are doing something that is not His plan for our lives, He will step in and change things.
- God calls us to be different – have integrity – trust Him.
- There are always consequences to our sin – we are forgiven but there are still repercussions to our actions.

- Our lives are representative of the God we serve. If we act like the rest of the unbelieving world, why would people want to come to Christ?
- We need to learn to do the right thing regardless of our fears.

The first dot we want to connect is that God will change a person's heart to move us to the place He wants us. We learned this lesson through our son Jesse. When Jesse was in High School he was dating Hannah. He met her at church and they were crazy about each other for a couple years. Before they both went off to college they broke up and went different directions. She went to a college in Arizona and Jesse went back to Illinois. I (Lisa) always felt they were meant for each other but Rob was convinced Jesse should focus on his school without any distractions back home.

After they both graduated Jesse came home one day and said he heard Hannah was probably going to get married soon since she had gotten back with an old boyfriend. I was devastated since I was convinced they should be together. Jesse didn't seem to be interested, at the time, but I couldn't shake the feeling they should be together so I decided to start praying. I would get on my knees at night and I would cry and I would pray and I would beg God that if these two were to be together then He had to work a miracle. He would have to rekindle the love they once shared, He would have to open their eyes to each other and He would have to somehow bring them back together.

A couple weeks later I was at the office talking to Jesse and he had a strange look on his face. I started asking him about different girls he had been talking to and if he was interested in them and he finally said "Mom, I don't know what is wrong with me but I can't stop thinking about Hannah." I decided that this relationship had to be totally God's deal and not mine so I decided I would not say anything to Rob about this until he asked and so I prayed the Holy Spirit would move on his heart to bring up Hannah. A couple days later,

Rob and I went to lunch and as we were talking he asked me what was wrong with Jesse! I told him it was probably girls and he specifically asked if this was about Hannah! As we talked, he said Jesse should pursue her and give this relationship a try if he was feeling this way.

Unbeknownst to us, Hannah's mom was doing the exact thing. A few months before, she started feeling the same way I had been feeling and so she was praying just as fervently as I was! Hannah ended the relationship she was in with her boyfriend, she and Jesse got back together and last week they were married! Nobody could be more thrilled than all of the parents! This has been a great testimony of how God changes hearts on His timing and in His ways.

Getting back to the story of Abraham, we see how God changed Pharoah's heart to release Sarai even though Abraham was in the wrong, God continued to keep he and Sarai safe all the while. God is the One who is our protector in life, even when we do things that are not really that smart. On the property we live, there is an old mine in the mountain. When our boys were younger (we assume we were not home since we would never let them do this) they decided to go into the mine with their BB gun. They thought it would be funny to shoot the bats in a small enclosed area while they were standing there. This would be one of the many times in our lives that God has protected our boys even when they were doing really dumb things!

We have to remember the all powerful God we serve. He knows our every move and our every dumb mistake and yet, as His children, He protects us just like He did for Abraham. Just like Abraham, there are serious consequences to the things we do that go against God's call on our lives and yet He is always faithful to forgive us and teach us valuable lessons along the way.

The second dot to connect is the fact that our behavior really does matter. The Egyptian people were probably turned *away* from

God instead of *to* God because of Abraham's actions. We want to stand for our faith with honor and integrity in hopes that people will see our lives and come to Christ. I (Rob) was invited to a Bible Study by a man who had an incredible ministry in the area. I looked up to this man; he was like a mentor to me. He had a beautiful family and an ongoing ministry for kids and even wrote books. One day, his life started on a downward spiral as a friendship turned to an affair which destroyed his marriage and his ministry. The devastation this brought to those watching this man destroy his life and his ministry was incalculable.

We have to remember that people are watching us. If we claim to be followers of Jesus, our lives must reflect what we say we believe. How many times do we hear of people who refuse to come to Christ because of the hypocrisy they see in other people? We have to reflect on our own lives at work, at the gym, at school, with family, friends or at home. Regardless of where we are, we have to remember our Christian walk must shine through. Since we have four boys that are married now, we had to go through the normal wedding functions like bachelor parties. As this last one approached, we had to remind the boys not to forget they were Christians first! Sometimes we forget that others are watching us.

The third dot to connect is the fact there are always consequences to our sin. If a person commits adultery the cost could be losing their family and destroying trust. If a person is dishonest at work they could get fired. If a person kills someone they will spend the rest of their life in prison. If a person is a drug addict or alcoholic it could destroy the relationships in their life. God wants to show us how important it is to obey His commands and live life with honor without ever having to look over our shoulder. God gives us His Word to help us make wise decisions so we can live a life of peace. Sin brings sorrow while doing the right thing brings a life of calmness and serenity.

Abraham is a great reminder we can trust God through the

difficult moments. If you are confused – pray. Wait on God. Talk to people who have the gift of wisdom. Read your Bible so God can speak to you and then do what you feel He is leading you to do. When we trust Him we can also trust He will open the right doors and close the wrong ones. If we are seeking what He wants for our lives then we can have the confidence He will move us in the direction He wants us to go.

Remember this: **Romans 8:14 says: "For all who are being led by the Spirit of God, these are sons of God."** God promises that as a Christian we have the Holy Spirit living inside of us, guiding us where we are supposed to go. We cannot imagine living a life without His guidance. We cannot imagine living a life without the knowledge of God who is leading and guiding our lives. We have a purpose in our lives and God wants us to learn how to trust His guiding hand and learn to hear his voice.

Dots to Connect

- We are not immune to trouble in our lives.

- When trouble comes our way we must recognize God has not skipped out on us.

- God always has a purpose for our trials.

- We need to learn to trust God and be patient as we wait on Him to show us what He is doing.

- Our faith cannot depend upon what God does or does not do for us.

- We must learn to be "even if" kind of people, knowing God is still in control even if our prayers are not answered the way we would like.

- We need to remember how God has taken care of us in the past to help us grow our faith for the future.

- Our behavior really does matter.

- God changes hearts to move us where He wants us.

- There are always consequences to sin.

Chapter 4

Regarding Sin

When God first called Abraham he was living in a place called Ur which is modern day Iraq. God called him to move to the land of Canaan which is modern day Israel. When the famine hit, Abraham decided to go to Egypt and when he had lied about his wife to Pharaoh and was escorted out of town – Abraham had a choice. Should he go back to Ur? Should he forget this whole "God thing" and just go home? Many times when we sin and get caught, our flinch is to run. We want away from the people we hurt, we want to never been seen by the people we embarrassed. However, the great thing about Abraham is he went back to the land God had promised him. He faced his sin and moved on with life.

People can get stuck in the past, but God is the God of the future. For Abraham, the long ride home from Egypt was probably a difficult ride. He had to make it right with Sariah, he had to make it right with the family and friends he had taken with him. The slaves given to him by Pharaoh probably had a twisted view of God because of Abraham's actions. Instead of running away, Abraham seemed to face his failure and move on.

If you have been devastated by sin in your past, God wants you to move on. Seek the forgiveness from those you have hurt, and do what **Philippians 3:13-14** says: **"Brethren, I do not regard myself as having laid hold of it yet; but one thing I do: forgetting what lies behind and reaching forward to what lies ahead, I press on toward the goal for the prize of the upward call of God in Christ Jesus."** When a person becomes a Christian, he does so because he recognizes there is a huge chasm between himself and God. We can never be good enough, on our own, to reach God and our sin is what keeps us from a relationship with Him. Fortunately, in the incredible plan of God, He sent Jesus to die on a cross and take our sins upon Himself and now He alone bridges the gap between us and God. **Psalm 103:12** says: **"As far as the east is from the west, so far has He removed our transgressions from us."**

When we refuse to deal with our sin, it affects everything in our life. When David, in the Old Testament, had an affair with Bathsheba and had her husband killed on the front lines, he recognized one thing. **Psalm 32:3-5** says: **"When I kept silent about my sin, my body wasted away through my groaning all day long. For day and night Your hand was heavy upon me; my vitality was drained away as with the fever heat of summer. I acknowledged my sin to You, and my iniquity I did not hide; I said, I will confess my transgressions to the Lord; and You forgave the guilt of my sin."** **Psalm 38:3** adds **"There is no soundness in my flesh because of Your indignation; There is no health in my bones because of my sin."**

If you are dealing with sin in your life, confess it, acknowledge it to God, repent and move on. Abraham seems to have done just that. Instead of running away, he went back to where God called him. We have to realize we are all human and many can and do fall into serious sin but God continued to love Abraham and bless him. God had a plan for Abraham's life and even his sin could not thwart His purposes. Sin teaches us about ourselves and about God's faithfulness. Do not let past sin become so debilitating that you cannot move forward in your life. God wanted Abraham back in the Promised Land and Abraham faced his failure and moved on with his life.

This is why we can forget our sins and our past; He removes them and forgets them. They are paid for. Our slate is wiped clean. **Psalm 25:7 says: "Do not remember the sins of my youth or my transgressions; according to Your lovingkindness remember me, for Your goodness sake, O Lord."**

The dot we want to connect, here, is the fact that God can use our past for His purposes. Who better to help someone through the devastating effects of an adulterous affair than someone whose life had been destroyed by the same thing? Who better to help someone work through divorce than someone who has been through it? Who better to teach someone the art of forgiveness than from someone who has been forgiven much? We have a friend who has a family member addicted to drugs. At the moment, they feel devastated, and yet they know God could change this person's life in a moment's time. They pray, they talk, and then they pray more. What they do know is that God can use this situation in mighty ways. If this person walks away from the destructive lifestyle he is in and comes back to the Lord, his parents know what kind of incredible testimony he will have. If he doesn't and God has a different plan, they are learning to completely trust their child's life to God. For many people, they can only see what is in front of them – drugs, sadness, and dysfunction. For these parents they see ministry: helping other parents in the same situation.

We need to remember God may be using our past sin or our family situations to help others grow in their relationship with Him. We cannot run from our past, we must face it, repent of it and move on to the life God has for us. That is what we can learn from Abraham as he returns from his sin in Egypt just as we learned from David and his sin with Bathsheba.

Psalm 51, A Psalm of David, when Nathan the prophet came to him, after he had gone in to Bathsheba. "Be gracious to me, O God, according to Your lovingkindness; According to the greatness of Your compassion blot out my transgressions. Wash me

thoroughly from my iniquity and cleanse me from my sin. For I know my transgressions, and my sin is ever before me. Against You, You only, I have sinned and done what is evil in Your sight, So that You are justified when You speak And blameless when You judge. Behold, I was brought forth in iniquity, and in sin my mother conceived me. Behold, You desire truth in the innermost being, And in the hidden part You will make me know wisdom. Purify me with hyssop, and I shall be clean; Wash me, and I shall be whiter than snow. Make me to hear joy and gladness, Let the bones which You have broken rejoice. Hide Your face from my sins And blot out all my iniquities. Create in me a clean heart, O God, and renew a steadfast spirit within me. Do not cast me away from Your presence And do not take Your Holy Spirit from me. Restore to me the joy of Your salvation And sustain me with a willing spirit. Then I will teach transgressors Your ways, And sinners will be converted to You. Deliver me from bloodguiltiness, O God, the God of my salvation; Then my tongue will joyfully sing of Your righteousness. O Lord, open my lips, That my mouth may declare Your praise. For You do not delight in sacrifice, otherwise I would give it; You are not pleased with burnt offering. The sacrifices of God are a broken spirit; A broken and a contrite heart, O God, You will not despise. By Your favor do good to Zion; Build the walls of Jerusalem. Then You will delight in righteous sacrifices, In burnt offering and whole burnt offering; Then young bulls will be offered on Your altar."

Dots to Connect

- Face your failures and move on.

- Do not let past sin become so debilitating that you cannot move forward.

- God can use our past mistakes for His purpose

Chapter 5

Family Problems

Most of Abraham's life, as we will see, he struggled with family problems. The first problem we encounter after his ordeal in Egypt with his wife Sarah will be his nephew Lot. When Abraham moved to the Promised Land, his nephew Lot came along with him. Between the two, they both amassed great amounts of wealth; flocks, herds and tents. The land that Abraham was on could not hold both of them so Abraham went to Lot.

Genesis 13:8-9 says: So Abram said to Lot, "Please let there be no strife between you and me, nor between my herdsmen and your herdsmen, for we are brothers. Is not the whole land before you? Please separate from me; if to the left, then I will go to the right; or if to the right, then I will go to the left."

Abraham seems to have learned something from his time in Egypt – his selfish concern for his own life turned to care and concern for others. Abraham was older and the land was promised to him but he allowed Lot, his selfish nephew, to choose first where he wanted to live.

**Genesis 13:10-11 says: "Lot lifted up his eyes and saw all the valley of the Jordan, that it was well watered everywhere—this was before the Lord destroyed Sodom and Gomorrah—like the garden of the Lord, like the land of Egypt as you go to Zoar. So Lot chose for himself all the valley of the Jordan, and Lot journeyed eastward. Thus they separated from each other."

Abraham connected this dot: God would move Lot's heart where He wanted him. Abraham did not need to talk Lot into taking the worst land – he only needed to trust that God would move Lot to where He was supposed to be. Abraham was learning what faith is – trusting God for the outcome even if it doesn't seem right. The land Lot chose was in the valley where the Jordon River ran through it. If you look at pictures of this area it was green and lush and well watered. The land Abraham was stuck with was nothing like where Lot moved to and yet what we see in Abraham's life is contentment. He never seems angry with Lot or frustrated with his choice. He had learned to sit back and trust that God has a purpose for even things that seem unfair in life.

Family can be difficult. So many feelings get attached to our parents, brothers, sisters, children and grandchildren. There is always the chance our feeling will get hurt. If someone doesn't come to a family event, we are sad. If someone forgets to call on a birthday, it ruins the day. Abraham learned a great lesson that we all should learn where family is concerned – life is not always about us. If we can connect this dot – our family relationships will be peaceful and filled with joy. When we learn to care more for others than our own "rights" – we can walk through life without the sadness and strife so many family issues can cause.

The dot we need to connect is what Abraham learned – where there is a problem, go talk it out. **Matthew 18:15, "If your brother sins, go and show him his fault in private; if he listens to you, you have won your brother."** The problem with many families is that nobody wants to talk about hurt feelings. They want to keep it stuffed inside them and it only festers and causes worse feelings as time goes on. Abraham learned to deal with the issue at hand. We need to learn to sit down face to face with people we have issues with. Unfortunately, technology seems to hurt us in this area. It is much easier to vent our feelings to someone over a voice mail or e-mail but unfortunately, it is difficult to share feelings and emotions without being in personal contact.

We have seven children and the three middle boys are very close in age. One Thanksgiving two of the boys got in a huge argument and they couldn't seem to solve it so I (Rob) stepped in. We sat them down and had them talk out their problems in order to clear the air between the two of them. We have always instilled in our children the importance of never allowing problems to come between us as a family – we have seen so many situations where families break apart because one or both parties refuse to sit down and talk it out. By the end of the night, both boys apologized to each other, hugged each other and moved on. That is why the most important thing to do, when there are family issues, is to talk through them.

Abraham understood this. He had a few choices to make; he could have ignored the problem or he could have talked to everyone behind Lot's back. These are both serious issues. By ignoring the problem, it causes more friction but could also lead to gossip. Lot could have started rumors about Abraham and his herdsman could pass that on down the line. Now instead of conflict between just Lot and Abraham, there is now strife with their employees.

Gossip is always divisive. Nothing ever good comes out of spreading rumors because as we all know – what starts out as something minor always grows. Gossip is always negative and for some reason people love to hear gossip. Somehow by hearing unconstructive things about others makes us feel better about ourselves. There is something about having information on others that makes us feel more powerful.

The Bible says in **Proverbs 20:19, "He who goes about as a slanderer reveals secrets, therefore do not associate with a** gossip" and in **Proverbs 16:28, "A perverse man spreads strife, and a slanderer separates intimate friends."**

Abraham could have destroyed Lot by his words to others. We never see Abraham angry or upset that Lot took the best land. That would have been great grounds for gossip and yet Abraham refused to go there. All of this comes back to connecting the dot regarding faith. Abraham trusted God and he knew Lot's decision was from the Lord.

Proverbs 16:33 says: "The lot is cast into the lap, but its every decision is from the Lord."

When we start putting things into an eternal perspective, there never is a reason to talk bad about someone else.God is in control; He moves on hearts, He uses all situations to teach us something. Maybe God is teaching us to be kind and loving to others, maybe He wants us to have faith He is still in control. If Lot wanted the best land, that was cause for Abraham to rejoice because his trust was in God – not Lot. We have to be so careful what we say about people. Our immediate thought should be to pray for the person instead of talk behind their back to others.

We need to learn to not take life so serious. People say hurtful things they do not really mean. People have difficult days. People get angry and frustrated in life. Usually a day or two later things are back to normal. When we can connect the dot to help those who are upset instead of hurt them, then strife will cease. Abraham did just this. He took what Lot did to him and knew somehow it was from God so he could be at peace. If someone hurts you, go talk it out with them – not others. Know God is using the situation for some reason in your life. Just like Abraham, we need to pray that we can love our family members more than we love ourselves.

Proverbs 21:23, "He who guards his mouth and his tongue, guards his soul from troubles."

Proverbs 26:20-21, "For lack of wood the fire goes out, and where there is no whisperer, contention quiets down. Like charcoal to hot embers and wood to fire, so is a contentious man to kindle strife."

Lot would eventually learn some valuable lessons in his life. Because of this selfish choice he made he would, in the long run, lose much more than he ever gained.

Genesis 13:13 says, "Now the men of Sodom were wicked exceedingly and sinners against the Lord."

Instead of Lot looking out for the welfare of his family and who his children's friends would be, he focused on the things that would make him wealthy. He moved his family to a very wicked city that God would eventually destroy. Once Lot moved away, God showed up to Abraham to remind him, once again, the land around him would be his.

Genesis 13:14-18, The Lord said to Abram, after Lot had separated from him, "Now lift up your eyes and look from the place where you are, northward and southward and eastward and westward; for all the land which you see, I will give it to you and to your descendants forever. I will make your descendants as the dust of the earth, so that if anyone can number the dust of the earth, then your descendants can also be numbered. Arise, walk about the land through its length and breadth; for I will give it to you." Then Abram moved his tent and came and dwelt by the oaks of Mamre, which are in Hebron, and there he built an altar to the Lord.

Wherever there are families – there are always occasions for problems. As Christians, we have to learn like Abraham, that God needs to be in the midst. We have to learn to love others more than ourselves. We have to learn that God moves us to different places in life and sometimes He uses family to do that. We have to learn that when it seems we are getting the bad end of a deal; God is still in control. We need to be reminded that it doesn't matter what others do to us but it does matter what our response is to them. The Bible makes it clear in the following verse that if you feel persecuted or hurt by your family, God's remedy is to love them and pray for them. Think about this every time a situation comes up where you feel hurt.

Matthew 5:44-45, "But I say to you, love your enemies and pray for those who persecute you, so that you may be sons of your Father who is in heaven; for He causes His sun to rise on the evil and the good, and sends rain on the righteous and the unrighteous."

God is faithful even when we feel a wrong has been done to us. If someone in your family has hurt you, please go make it right. The dot we want to connect is the fact that in every situation, good or bad, God is still in it. He is always trying to teach us to look more like Jesus each day. In order for that to happen, there will always be conflict, trials and temptations. We know people who have gone through devastating divorces and yet years later we see the spiritual growth that occurred because of heartache. God uses sad things to teach us compassion, hurtful things to teach us to forgive, frustrating circumstances to teach us to trust. If all our lives we never had any problems, how could we learn to be like Jesus?

Dots to Connect

- God is still in control even when the situation seems unfair.

- If you have a problem with someone – go and talk it out with them.

- When things do not go our way – instead of gossip we need to learn to trust that God is still working, even through the hurt and pain others may cause us.

- Do not take life so serious – people have bad days and say things they really do not mean.

- Love others more than we love ourselves and strife will subside.

- It doesn't matter what others do to us; but it does matter how we respond to them.

- God uses sad things to teach us compassion, hurtful things to teach us forgiveness, and frustrating circumstances to teach us to trust Him.

- God is faithful and has a purpose even when we feel wrong has been done to us.

Chapter 6

Trials and Faith

The Bible says in **James 1:2-4, "Consider it all joy, my brethren, when you encounter various trials, knowing that the testing of your faith produces endurance. And let endurance have its perfect result, so that you may be perfect and complete, lacking in nothing."** Consider it joy when things go wrong? There is nothing we like about difficult times coming into our lives and yet, God says it is those things that will teach us to persevere. What if we could be joyful when a spouse walks out the door, a child becomes a drug addict or we just lost a job? What if we could see God's hand in every event in our lives? Wouldn't that change how we respond to heartache? Wouldn't we walk through life with a peace and joy knowing EVERYTHING brought into our lives is from Him to teach us something?

That is where God wants us. He doesn't want us to think of Him as this distant God that shows up on Sundays but instead, He is the God who is intimately involved in every part of our lives. Think about how this should transform our daily thought patterns. At work when we do not get the account we have been working on, instead of falling apart we thank God that He evidently knew something we didn't know. Maybe this particular job would have bankrupted the company. Maybe this particular client would have done more harm than good for you. God can see the future; we can't.

What happens when your wife is not the wife you thought you married? What happens when your husband stops being the loving attentive person you said, "I do" to? What happens when your spouse is selfish or rude or jealous or possessive? Do you walk out the door? Do you give up on the vows you made? The Bible says, "no" and instead asks us to consider it joy. Difficult? We would venture to say, "impossible."

The greatest thing about God is the promise in **Matthew 19:26, And looking at them Jesus said to them, "With people this is impossible, but with God all things are possible."** The world wants us to run from our problems but Jesus wants us to recognize that "all" things are possible. We have seen incredible life changes that we never, in a million years, would think God could do. We have seen Him save people who wanted nothing to do with Him. We have seen Him put back together marriages that seemed totally hopeless. We have seen prisoners get out of prison and serve God the rest of their lives. This is the God we serve – the God of the impossible! So, what happens when we have to wait years and years for things to change? What do we do in the meantime?

Consider it joy. Joy is one of those things that is produced by the Holy Spirit living in our lives. Happiness is based on our circumstances where joy is dependent on trusting God. Joy is available to us as we draw closer and closer to God, knowing He is growing us up to look more like Him. **Hebrews 12:2** says, **"fixing our eyes on Jesus, the author and perfecter of faith, who for the joy set before Him endured the cross, despising the shame, and has sat down at the right hand of the throne of God."**

Jesus is our perfect example of a life filled with pain. People refused to believe He was God, they used Him, they spat on Him, they mocked Him and ultimately beat Him, scourged Him and crucified Him. Through it all – there was joy because He looked past today and focused on eternity. That is why we can have joy – this world does not end here. As believers in Jesus, we have forever in eternity to look forward to and we can be joyous in all circumstances knowing we are only here for a short time. Yes, life is difficult with many trials and yet, trials move us on to a life of trusting Him with all of our situations. That is why we can have joy.

What happens at home when you learn your child has been doing drugs? Did God turn His back for a minute and didn't see this trial coming in your life? No way. Maybe He has a plan for your life that involves teaching kids about drug prevention. Maybe your child will eventually see the foolishness of his ways and have a ministry to help others. We never know what God has in store for our lives but when we give our lives to Him, we are giving control to Him. As a Christian, our daily lives are not separate from our faith; we have to know they are connected.

We have a friend whose husband is an alcoholic. She is a Christian and he is not. Instead of feeling sorry for herself she feels she has a ministry to help others understand alcoholism and help children deal with parents suffering from this disease. She is using this trial in her life as a ministry for God. She is persevering; she is staying with her husband. Many people tell her she should leave, find someone else, why waste her life? If God is involved then she looks at her trials differently; not as the world does but as God does. God is giving her the strength to live like this and she knows she can help others who are dealing with the same thing.

James 1:12, "Blessed is a man who perseveres under trial; for once he has been approved, he will receive the crown of life which the Lord has promised to those who love Him."

1 Peter 1:6-7, "In this you greatly rejoice, even though now for a little while, if necessary, you have been distressed by various trials, so that the proof of your faith, being more precious than

gold which is perishable, even though tested by fire, may be found to result in praise and glory and honor at the revelation of Jesus Christ."

We cannot separate our lives from our faith. The world will always tell us to handle problems differently than God does. The world wants us to think our lives are about us, we should be angry if things don't go our way, and we should get back at people who hurt us. However, as Christians, God is calling us to be different. If our life and faith were two separate entities, it would make sense to challenge all the bad that happens to us. When our faith and life are connected, we see our trials in a completely new light. We rejoice when bad things happen because we trust God is doing something in our lives. We refuse to gossip about someone who hurt us because we know God calls us to forgive. We can see tragedy in our lives as an opportunity to learn to trust God even though we cannot see any reason for what is happening.

When we can learn to connect this dot, everything in our lives will change. No longer will we fall apart when something bad happens because we know He is in control. No longer will we be anxious about finances because we will learn to trust Him to provide. No longer will we be heartbroken if a boyfriend or girlfriend breaks up with us because we will know God is protecting us from this person. When we can insert God into every situation, we can walk through life with a peace and joy that those in the world cannot experience. When this dot is connected, our lives will never be the same.

Ephesians 5:15, "Therefore be careful how you walk, not as unwise men but as wise... "

As we come back to the story of Abraham, he is getting ready to be forced into a problem that he would have no control over and, again, his crazy nephew Lot would be right in the middle of it. Sodom and Gomorrah were located at the southern end of the Salt Sea in the land of Canaan and for some reason the Kings of these towns were paying an assessed tribute to King Chedorlaomer – King of Elam. When the Kings of Sodom and Gomorrah decided not to pay the King of Elam anymore, a war ensued and Lot was caught right in the middle. This mighty army that came from modern day Iraq and modern day Iran came down into modern day Israel to get what was owed to them. As Lot's town was trying to defend themselves this is what happened:

Genesis 14:10-12, "Now the valley of Siddim was full of tar pits; and the kings of Sodom and Gomorrah fled, and they fell into them. But those who survived fled to the hill country. Then they took all the goods of Sodom and Gomorrah and all their food supply, and departed. They also took Lot, Abram's nephew, and his possessions and departed, for he was living in Sodom."

Lot and his family were kidnapped and this is how Abraham found out:

Genesis 14:13, "Then a fugitive came and told Abram the Hebrew. Now he was living by the oaks of Mamre the Amorite, brother of Eshcol and brother of Aner, and these were allies with Abram."

Abraham had a choice – should he help rescue Lot, the crazy nephew who selfishly took the best land from him? Should he just assume God was paying him back for what he did? How would we respond? Would we help someone who had hurt us?

Feeling sorry for ourselves • • •

Sometimes when we have difficulty with people or additional stress in our lives we tend to feel sorry for ourselves. For Abraham, he had a choice. He could have fallen into a depression because the force against him was too overwhelming. He could have decided the job to save Lot was too intense. He could have remembered how Lot took the best land for himself. All of these feelings could have moved him away from helping Lot. Instead, he got his focus off of himself and put his focus on helping others.

I (Rob) was having a day like this a few weeks ago, as I was driving home, I wanted to get home and shut out the world. I just happened to call a friend of mine who is a pastor in a town where he serves the poor. As he was explaining his day to me, I realized that my bad day didn't even compare to his. I learned, once again, that when I focus on myself and my pain and my hurts, and my bad day; I can easily forget there is a world that is hurting more than I could ever be.

I was talking to one of our children, one day, in regards to his life. He was feeling down about things that were going on and I told him to go find a ministry to get involved with. He decided to start a ministry where he would collect coats and jackets for the homeless and he and his wife did just that. He was amazed at how different he felt when he got the focus off of himself and on to others.

When we get depressed, we start looking inward and how bad our lives are but when we can get outside of ourselves and help others, our focus changes. Jesus served others regardless of how exhausted he was. He cared for others knowing the pain He would suffer on the cross. He gave his life away for others in the midst of sadness, heartache and sickness. Thankfully, for us, He lived His life as a service to others.

Just like Abraham, we need to recognize we live in a world where people will hurt us. We need to keep in mind we live in a world where circumstances can overwhelm us; we will lose jobs, get sick, and not have money to pay our bills. That is real life. When these things happen, we need to remember to look outward on serving others instead of looking inward focusing on ourselves. The life of a believer is one that imitates Christ and nowhere do we see Jesus worrying about Himself. He was here to serve others regardless of His circumstances.

Abraham was a great example of this. Instead of sitting around feeling sorry for himself because Lot had taken the best land he, in spite of this, took his time, energy and his trained soldiers to go out and save and serve the very person who had acted selfishly toward him! That is what being a Christian is all about – doing what God is calling us to do regardless of what others have done to us. That could mean:

Being kind to an ex-spouse
Calling a wayward child to tell them you love them
Taking the person who gossiped about you out for coffee
Helping someone at work who never helps you
Praying for someone who hurt you deeply
Doing something kind for your spouse that you would normally not do

Just like Abraham, our love for God and doing what He asks of us must override our negative feelings toward people. God will always place people and circumstances in our lives to help us grow in our faith. How do we respond when we are hurt? Hopefully, we can learn from Abraham how to care for others regardless of how they have treated us.

Once again, we see Abraham putting aside any negative feelings and instead of ignoring the problem, he got his army together and went after Lot.

Genesis 14:14-16, "When Abram heard that his relative had been taken captive, he led out his trained men, born in his house, three hundred and eighteen, and went in pursuit as far as Dan. He divided his forces against them by night, he and his servants, and defeated them, and pursued them as far as Hobah, which is north of Damascus. He brought back all the goods, and also brought back his relative Lot with his possessions, and also the women, and the people."

Three hundred and eighteen trained men. For some reason that doesn't seem like a lot of men to go up against an army of four kings; which brings us to the point that God is in charge of fighting our battles for us. When we can connect this dot – we will pray more, trust more, and seek God more. Our problem is we are used to fighting our own battles. We can talk to the right bankers, invest in the right investments and make our decisions in our business. But, when we can step aside, work diligently and recognize that God is fighting our battles for us; it will change our lives.

When we get down about the economy and our financial situation, our first reaction is to panic. What should we do? How can we get money to continue our business? Should we raise prices? Should we lower prices? What about adding more salespeople? All of these are valid questions and our prayer is that God will give us the wisdom to make the right choices. However, that is the difference; no longer are we working through these problems alone. We are consulting God, knowing He is in the midst of these battles with us. We trust Him to help us make good decisions. We are connecting the dots between the battles we face each day and our relationship to God. **2 Chronicles 20** is our favorite place to go when we feel desperate and do not know where to turn. We start to remember that the battle is the Lord's.

2 Chronicles 20:1-2, "Now it came about after this that the sons of Moab and the sons of Ammon, together with some of the Meunites, came to make war against Jehoshaphat. Then some came and reported to Jehoshaphat, saying, 'A great multitude is coming against you from beyond the sea, out of Aram and behold, they are in Hazazon-tamar (that is Engedi).'"

How would we feel if we heard "a great multitude is coming against you"? Probably fear and panic would arise. For us, instead of an army coming against us it could be things like:

- I lost my job and I can't afford to make a house payment

- I lost our largest account at work
- Our investment account has been frozen and we have no way of getting money to live on
- My husband or wife is walking out the door
- My child has been in an accident
- I just found out I have cancer
- The bank is repossessing my house and we have nowhere to go
- Electricity is being shut off today and I have no money to pay the bill
- My 401K has been depleted and I have to start over.

Just like Jehoshaphat hearing a great multitude was coming against him, we have the same feelings as he did.

2 Chronicles 20:3, "Jehoshaphat was afraid and turned his attention to seek the Lord, and proclaimed a fast throughout all Judah."

The greatest part of the Bible is the honesty of the men. Here was a powerful King who was faced with an impossible situation and was sincere enough to tell us how he felt; he was afraid. We all get afraid sometimes because we all are human. Fear is an emotion which unchecked could be harmful, but what Jehoshaphat does is what we should all do. Instead of running away from God he turned his attention to Him. His fear moved Him to seek God which is what we need to do.

Jehoshaphat prayed to God an amazing prayer, while all along He reminded himself of the power of God. Sometimes we forget that God created everything, He holds every moment of our lives in His hands, He moves on hearts, He changes people and He changes circumstances. Sometimes it is in the fearful times that we need to remember.

2 Chronicles 20:6-9, and he said, "O Lord, the God of our fathers, are You not God in the heavens? And are You not ruler

over all the kingdoms of the nations? Power and might are in Your hand so that no one can stand against You. Did You not, O our God, drive out the inhabitants of this land before Your people Israel and give it to the descendants of Abraham Your friend forever? They have lived in it, and have built You a sanctuary there for Your name, saying, 'Should evil come upon us, the sword, or judgment, or pestilence, or famine, we will stand before this house and before You (for Your name is in this house) and cry to You in our distress, and You will hear and deliver us.'"

As Jehoshaphat was praying he seems to be reminding God that he knows who He is. He recognizes these things:

- You are God in heaven
- You are ruler over all the kingdoms and nations
- You are powerful
- You are mighty
- Nobody could ever stand against You
- You drove out the inhabitants of the land of Israel and gave it to Abraham's descendants
- We will cry out to You in distress
- You will hear us and deliver us

Jehoshaphat also recognizes these facts:
2 Chronicles 20:12, "O our God, will You not judge them? For we are powerless before this great multitude who are coming against us; nor do we know what to do, but our eyes are on You."

2 Chronicles 20:15, and he said, "Listen, all Judah and the inhabitants of Jerusalem and King Jehoshaphat: thus says the Lord to you, 'Do not fear or be dismayed because of this great multitude, for the battle is not yours but God's.'"

That is what we need to learn to do – recognize the battle is His. We can work diligently at our jobs and raise our children with integrity but we are powerless for the outcome. God alone is the One who will fight our battles for us. He alone will move on our children's hearts to seek Him. We are human and powerless to change situations at work – only He can. When we come to this realization – another dot is connected. Now our work, our children and grandchildren, we recognize, are out of our control. We recognize our eyes have to be trained on Him alone to make things right. We spend our days praying and trusting the God who alone holds the key to our battles.

That does not mean we do not work hard at our jobs. The Bible is very specific regarding our willingness to work. We will be poor if we do not work. We will not have food on the table if we do not work. We work and pray for God's blessing upon what we do but ultimately we know that He controls it all.

Proverbs 10:4, "Poor is he who works with a negligent hand, but the hand of the diligent makes rich."

Proverbs 16:3, "Commit your works to the Lord and your plans will be established."

Proverbs 21:25, "The desire of the sluggard puts him to death, for his hands refuse to work."

2 Thessalonians 3:8-11, "nor did we eat anyone's bread without paying for it, but with labor and hardship we kept working night and day so that we would not be a burden to any of you; not because we do not have the right to this, but in order to offer ourselves as a model for you, so that you would follow our example. For even when we were with you, we used to give you this order: if anyone is not willing to work, then he is not to eat, either. For we hear that some among you are leading an undisciplined life, doing no work at all, but acting like busybodies."

As far as our children are concerned we are to train them up to know God. We need to teach them to connect the dots between their lives and their faith. Our youngest son plays basketball and our greatest desire is to teach him to be loving, caring and compassionate on the court. We want him to pass the ball and care more for others than himself. We try to teach him he has to live the faith he claims. We want his faith to be incorporated into his life on the basketball court as well as at school. We see some signs of this making sense in his life but until God reveals more and more of Himself to our son, we can only teach them and pray for them.

As our older boys started dating we wanted to help them connect the dots regarding this time in their lives. We wanted them to see how important it was to date Christian girls because the Bible says to not be unequally yoked. We wanted them to see a difference between someone who claimed to know Christ and someone who truly lived their faith. We knew dating could turn into marriage so that had to be a dot they needed to connect. We wanted them to choose a girl who loved the Lord with all their hearts because with God at the center of their relationship, we knew He would sustain them through anything.

We can pray for them, we can teach them the truths of God's Word and yet it is still up to God to fight these battles for us and change their hearts. We do our part and leave the rest to Him.

Psalm 78:5-7, "For He established a testimony in Jacob And appointed a law in Israel, which He commanded our fathers that they should teach them to their children, that the generation to come might know, even the children yet to be born, that they may arise and tell them to their children, that they should put their confidence in God and not forget the works of God, but keep His commandments."

Proverbs 22:6, "Train up a child in the way he should go, even when he is old he will not depart from it."

What we need to remember, as we close this chapter, is what God says to Jehoshaphat:

2 Chronicles 20:17, "You need not fight in this battle; station yourselves, stand and see the salvation of the Lord on your behalf, O Judah and Jerusalem. Do not fear or be dismayed; tomorrow go out to face them, for the Lord is with you."

Do not fear.
Stand and see what the Lord will do.
The Lord is with you.

When we can connect this dot between our trials and God, we can be at peace. We can trust Him for the things that come into our lives we have no control over. We can live our faith out in our day to day trials and when others see the peace of God, we can share with them the Source – God Himself in our lives.

Do not fear.
Stand and see what the Lord will do.
The Lord is with you.

Dots to Connect

- We can have peace and joy in our lives when we know God is using all things to help us grow in our relationship with Him.

- God is not a distant God but is intimately involved in all parts of our lives.

- Joy can only be produced by the Holy Spirit living in our lives.

- Happiness is based on circumstances where joy is dependent on trusting God alone.

- Joy is produced when we insert God in every situation.

- We live in a world where circumstances can overwhelm us; yet when we focus on Christ and serving others it takes the focus off of us and our problems.

- God places people and circumstances in our lives to help us grow in our faith.

- When we are fearful, we need to remember to keep our eyes on God and recognize the battle is His to fight for us.

Chapter 7

Regarding the Timing of God

Why does God always wait until the last minute to answer our prayers? When we pray for something urgent, why does He seem to take His time? Does God have a purpose behind waiting? Abraham was the perfect example of learning to wait on God; unfortunately instead of waiting he decided to take matters into his own hands. He is a great model for us as to what NOT to do!

When God called Abraham out of Ur to the land of Canaan, he was around 75 years old. God gave him a promise that a great nation would be built from his offspring. The problem was; Abraham did not have any children. Abraham had been living in the land of Canaan for approximately 15 years and even though God had given him the promise of an heir, his wife was still not pregnant. Not only was Abraham and Sarai past child bearing age but the promise of God seemed an impossibility. Through the story of Abraham and Sarai, God wants to show us He is the God of the impossible.

What seems impossible in your life? Financial issues? Pregnancy issues? Health issues? What about wayward children or non-believing family members? How about the impossibility of finding a job in an economic downturn? What do we do when we see no way out and yet God continually wants us to trust Him?

In the Bible we read a story about the life of Moses. Moses was born at a time when all the Hebrew baby boys were being put to death. His mother hid him and then sent him down the Nile River in a basket in hopes of saving his life. Because God is sovereignly in control of everything, it was that exact time that Pharaoh's daughter heard the baby crying and she decided to keep the child for herself. Moses grew up in Pharaoh's home with a privileged life until one day when he saw a fellow Hebrew being beaten.

Exodus 2:11-15, "Now it came about in those days, when Moses had grown up, that he went out to his brethren and looked on their hard labors; and he saw an Egyptian beating a Hebrew, one of his brethren. So he looked this way and that, and when he saw there was no one around, he struck down the Egyptian and hid him in the sand. He went out the next day, and behold, two Hebrews were fighting with each other; and he said to the offender, 'Why are you striking your companion?' But he said, 'Who made you a prince or a judge over us? Are you intending to kill me as you killed the Egyptian?' Then Moses was afraid and said, 'Surely the matter has become known.' When Pharaoh heard of this matter, he tried to kill Moses. But Moses fled from the presence of Pharaoh and settled in the land of Midian, and he sat down by a well."

Moses ran away in fear for his life but God had other plans; Moses would be instrumental in getting his fellow Hebrews out of Egypt and back to the land of Canaan that had been promised to them by God. God eventually comes to Moses in a burning bush and tells him he has a job for him:

Exodus 3:6-11, "He said also, 'I am the God of your father, the God of Abraham, the God of Isaac, and the God of Jacob.' Then Moses hid his face, for he was afraid to look at God. The Lord said, 'I have surely seen the affliction of My people who are in Egypt, and have given heed to their cry because of their taskmasters, for I am aware of their sufferings. So I have come down to

deliver them from the power of the Egyptians, and to bring them up from that land to a good and spacious land, to a land flowing with milk and honey, to the place of the Canaanite and the Hittite and the Amorite and the Perizzite and the Hivite and the Jebusite. Now, behold, the cry of the sons of Israel has come to Me; furthermore, I have seen the oppression with which the Egyptians are oppressing them. Therefore, come now, and I will send you to Pharaoh, so that you may bring My people, the sons of Israel, out of Egypt.' But Moses said to God, 'Who am I, that I should go to Pharaoh, and that I should bring the sons of Israel out of Egypt?'"

Moses stuttered his way through an argument with God, reminding Him how difficult it was to speak and how he was sure God had the wrong person for this job! However, in the end, Moses went and Pharaoh was not very happy to see him. Moses politely asked for the Hebrews or the Israelites (the Jewish nation of today) to be let go and allowed to go back to their land but Pharaoh kept refusing.

Exodus 4:21 explains why: **The Lord said to Moses, "When you go back to Egypt see that you perform before Pharaoh all the wonders which I have put in your power; but I will harden his heart so that he will not let the people go."**

Why would God do that? Why wouldn't He just move on Pharaoh's heart to let them go? Why go through the heartache of plagues with boils, flies, frogs, and hail? Why did it take plague after plague with the culmination of the death of the Egyptians first born to get Pharaoh to let them go?

Ultimately, God wants us to know He alone is God. He is powerful, He is mighty and He can do the impossible. If Pharaoh let the people go on the first plague, how could everyone see the hand of God? How would people ever know the true God and what He is capable of doing if He didn't take the time to prove it? That is why

God makes us wait. He wants us to learn to trust Him alone so when we do get that job, or get pregnant, or get healed; we know it had to be Him alone.

We have some friends who wanted a baby. They tried for years and her husband finally set a date to quit trying since they were getting older. All she could do was pray that God would make this happen and on the very last month they were going to try, she miraculously got pregnant. Guess who gets all the glory? God. She knows this precious gift is from Him alone. Would she feel the same way if she had gotten pregnant years ago? Would she be as incredibly grateful to God if she didn't have to wait? Probably not!

We are people who assume we do it all. We go to school to get a good education. To get the best jobs, we put together the best resumes. We have great children because we teach them the right way to live. We are healthy because we take good vitamins and exercise. Our businesses are prospering because we are brilliant. Then God steps in and the economy goes under. The jobs are not that easy to find, we start getting sick and our children start doing drugs. How good are we doing now? When God turns things around in our lives we need to recognize how much we really need Him. If God had not brought plague upon plague on the Egyptians, the Israelites would never have been able to see God at work. Sometimes it takes trials and tribulations to get God back to His rightful place in our lives – in charge of everything.

When Moses finally got the Israelites out and on their way to the Promised Land, they came upon a serious problem; the Red Sea. Suddenly, the excitement they felt to get out of Egypt was frustrated by a large body of water that there was no way around. Even though they had seen incredible power and salvation and deliverance out of Egypt – they seemed to forget God could make this right also. Don't we all do the same? We look back on our lives and see the incredible ways God has always come through for us and yet the problems we face today seem almost too difficult even for

Him! Isn't that crazy? We feel like each crisis that keeps piling up is like the Red Sea – impossible to go through or around. But God wants us to go through the problems, with Him in the lead.

The next thing that happens is hard to imagine – after everything Pharaoh has been through, he decides he wants to go after the Israelites and bring them back! Once again, God takes full responsibility for hardening Pharaoh's heart and He does it so the Egyptians will know He is the Lord. That seems to be a theme for Moses – God wants people to look to Him as the author of everything. By putting the Israelites in difficult places, it gives God the chance to show them His power. Without problems, fear and pain; nobody would ever see God for who He truly is. When the Israelites looked behind them what they saw struck sheer terror in them; the Egyptians were coming after them and all they could see was a large body of water in front of them. Gripped with fear and nowhere to go, they had only one option left to them; they cried out to the Lord. That, we believe, is where God wants all of us.

Exodus 14:3-10, "For Pharaoh will say of the sons of Israel, 'They are wandering aimlessly in the land; the wilderness has shut them in. Thus I will harden Pharaoh's heart, and he will chase after them; and I will be honored through Pharaoh and all his army, and the Egyptians will know that I am the Lord.' And they did so. When the king of Egypt was told that the people had fled, Pharaoh and his servants had a change of heart toward the people, and they said, 'What is this we have done, that we have let Israel go from serving us?' So he made his chariot ready and took his people with him; and he took six hundred select chariots, and all the other chariots of Egypt with officers over all of them. The Lord hardened the heart of Pharaoh, king of Egypt, and he chased after the sons of Israel as the sons of Israel were going out boldly. Then the Egyptians chased after them with all the horses and chariots of Pharaoh, his horsemen and his army, and they overtook them camping by the sea, beside Pi-hahiroth, in front of Baal-zephon. As Pharaoh drew near, the sons of Israel

looked, and behold, the Egyptians were marching after them, and they became very frightened; so the sons of Israel cried out to the Lord."

Because the economy is the way it is right now, what money we have left is in an investment account. It is all the money we have to live on and put into our company. I (Rob) called to get our money out a few weeks ago and was told some shocking news – our money would not be available for 1-2 years. I came home and told Lisa and we both just looked at each other with the deer in the headlights look – what are we going to do? The money we needed to make our house payment, car payments and to put into our company to keep it running was not available. That to us was like trying to cross the Red Sea without anywhere to go.

Sometimes, we think that is where God wants us; with nowhere to go. When we look back on this time, years and years from now, we will be able to tell our children one thing; God provided a way out. As of today, we have no idea how that will be, but we do trust He will do something. Lisa was telling me the other day how she realized her bank account was her idol. As long as she knew she had money, life was great. Then God changed it all and the prospect of not being able to pay a bill was frightening to her but it has strengthened both of our faith in God. We now have nowhere to turn except the one place we should be turning; to God. So we pray more, we pray for more faith to believe, we pray together, we pray separately and the best part is that we are no longer trusting ourselves or our bank account, but we are trusting Him.

That is where the Israelites are – the enemy is coming behind them. They were so excited and hopeful for a new life in the Promised Land and yet now all their dreams were about to be shattered as they would be ushered back to Egypt to be slaves again. Once again – God waits for the last minute to make things right. As they cry out to the Lord they have a few questions for Moses:

Exodus 14:11-20, "Then they said to Moses, 'Is it because there were no graves in Egypt that you have taken us away to die in the wilderness? Why have you dealt with us in this way, bringing us out of Egypt? Is this not the word that we spoke to you in Egypt, saying, Leave us alone that we may serve the Egyptians? For it would have been better for us to serve the Egyptians than to die in the wilderness.'"

They are confused about what is happening. God spent so much time getting them out of Egypt; but for what? To have them die there? Don't we all do this – we never understand what God is doing and just when we think things are going alright; something else happens! Yet, with each trial and problem – God is teaching us more and more about Him. He is teaching us more and more about His faithfulness. He is teaching us who really is in control of our lives.

Our new daughter in law was talking about life the other day. As a newly married couple, she and our son are learning the heartaches of financial pressures. They both have been dealing with some health issues which has brought to their mail box some unwanted bills. She was so cute when she asked us, "Is it going to always be like this?" Our answer was, "Unfortunately yes, and on the month you think you will finally get ahead, your dishwasher will break!" That, (we hated to tell her) is life.

Our Christian life is like that too. Just when we think we understand what God is doing or wanting to teach us, we get thrown another curve ball. What Moses told the Israelites is exactly what He wants us, thousands of years later, to hear also.

Exodus 14:13, "But Moses said to the people, 'Do not fear! Stand by and see the salvation of the Lord which He will accomplish for you today; for the Egyptians whom you have seen today, you will never see them again forever. The Lord will fight for you while you keep silent.'"

Once again, God wants us to know the same thing we learned in the previous chapter:

- Do not fear!
- Stand by and see the salvation of the Lord!
- He will accomplish this for you.
- The Lord will fight for you.

Exodus 14:14-18 Then the Lord said to Moses, "Why are you crying out to Me? Tell the sons of Israel to go forward. As for you, lift up your staff and stretch out your hand over the sea and divide it, and the sons of Israel shall go through the midst of the sea on dry land. As for Me, behold, I will harden the hearts of the Egyptians so that they will go in after them; and I will be honored through Pharaoh and all his army, through his chariots and his horsemen. Then the Egyptians will know that I am the Lord, when I am honored through Pharaoh, through his chariots and his horsemen."

That is exactly what happened. The sea divided, the Israelites walked through and as the Egyptians followed them through the dry land it was then that God released the water to drown the Egyptians. God tells Moses He will be honored because of this – the Egyptians will know He is the Lord. That is what trials do and that is what waiting on God does for us. Somehow we have bought into this idea the Christian life is pain free filled with happiness alone and yet, as we read the Bible, we see a different story. God uses trials and difficult times in order to show us who He is. Moses learned with each complicated issue that it was God who wanted to shine through. He wanted Moses to trust Him alone so He could prove to him who He was.

That is why He waits to the last minute. That is why it seems many times He has forgotten us and somehow has become deaf to our prayers. In reality, none of that is happening. What He is doing is building our faith, teaching us to trust Him and not ourselves, and ultimately showing us we need to give up our lives to Him completely. When He does come through at the very last minute with a job, or baby, or healing or bringing a wayward child home we recognize it is only Him. That is what He wants – for us to know Him and have faith in Him even at the eleventh hour when everything is falling apart. He always comes through and His timing is always perfect.

Tired of Waiting • • •

The trouble begins when we decide we don't want to wait anymore. For Abraham, his problems began when he heard God tell him he would have descendants but the dilemma was, he didn't have any children. He and Sarah were past child bearing age and the thought of being the father of a great nation didn't make any sense to him.

Genesis 15:2-7, Abram said, "'O Lord God, what will You give me, since I am childless, and the heir of my house is Eliezer of Damascus?' And Abram said, 'Since You have given no offspring to me, one born in my house is my heir.' Then behold, the word of the Lord came to him, saying, 'This man will not be your heir; but one who will come forth from your own body, he shall be your heir.' And He took him outside and said, 'Now look toward the heavens, and count the stars, if you are able to count them.' And He said to him, 'So shall your descendants be.' Then he believed in the Lord; and He reckoned it to him as righteousness. And He said to him, 'I am the Lord who brought you out of Ur of the Chaldeans, to give you this land to possess it.'"

Abraham was confused and assumed God would use his servant Eliezer to produce the heir. Since the child would be born from his servant, Abraham would consider the child his own. Since this was a custom in that day, Abraham started questioning God and wondered if this was the way He would give him a child. But God told Abraham that the promised heir would come from his own body even though he was past the age where this was possible. Remember – we serve the God of the impossible.

Just because:
Your marriage feels like there is no hope…
    You didn't get hired for the job…
        Your boyfriend or girlfriend broke up with you…
            You lost your job…
                You can't make your house payment…
This does not mean God is not in it!

He is always working in our lives, working behind the scenes to make things happen at the perfect time. Our problem is that many times while waiting on God – we start to rationalize. We begin to think His silence means we need to step in and do something. Most times, His silence means the timing is not right, but unfortunately for Sarai and Abraham, they started rationalizing.

Genesis 16:1-2, "Now Sarai, Abram's wife had borne him no children, and she had an Egyptian maid whose name was Hagar. So Sarai said to Abram, 'Now behold, the Lord has prevented me from bearing children. Please go in to my maid; perhaps I will obtain children through her.' And Abram listened to the voice of Sarai."

Sarai does what most of us do, from time to time; when we don't get the answer we want, we take matters into our own hands. For Sarai she was tired of waiting and since the custom of the day allowed for a maid to have children for her mistress, Sarai decided she should make this happen. The Bible gives us Abraham's response; the verse says he listened to the voice of Sarai. The difficulty in this verse is we don't know exactly what Abraham was thinking. It would make sense to us that Abraham rationalized, since up to this point God never says his child would come from Sarai; He only says it would come from him. We could see how he would listen to his wife but the problem is, the Bible never says he addresses God. Sarai offers her maid to Abraham and he just goes along with it. Did he pray about it? Did he ask God for His peace if this is how it was to be? Did he even acknowledge God in this situation?

Evidently they both were tired of waiting which is understandable – ten years was a long time. We need to put ourselves in this situation – what would we do? Would we continue to wait on God or rationalize our way out of our circumstances? Many people marry the wrong person because they are tired of waiting. Some divorce their spouse because they do not see the change they want immediately so they get tired of waiting and walk out the door. We are not immune to what Abraham did.

Genesis 16:3-8, "After Abram had lived ten years in the land of Canaan, Abram's wife Sarai took Hagar the Egyptian, her maid, and gave her to her husband Abram as his wife. He went in to Hagar, and she conceived; and when she saw that she had conceived, her mistress was despised in her sight. And Sarai said to Abram, 'May the wrong done me be upon you. I gave my maid into your arms, but when she saw that she had conceived, I was despised in her sight. May the Lord judge between you and me.' But Abram said to Sarai, 'Behold, your maid is in your power; do to her what is good in your sight.' So Sarai treated her harshly, and she fled from her presence."

By refusing to wait on God, the heartache in this family was devastating. Hagar treated Sarai with contempt and Sarai was jealous, angry and ruthless. The consequences of this sin reach the world today, over four thousand years later. Because of their refusal to wait on God, the fight in the Middle East continues on today. Ishmael, the son born by Hagar, is the lineage of the Arab nation. Isaac, who will be born to Abraham and Sarai, is the lineage of the people of Israel. The fight continues to this day and will continue until Jesus returns.

When we refuse to do what God asks of us, the dot we need to make sure and connect is that there are always negative consequences. Solomon is a great example of this in the Bible. When King David died, Solomon, his son took the throne. God promises a life of blessing to Solomon and his descendants; but for that to happen, Solomon would have to follow Him and obey His commands.

2 Chronicles 7:17-22, "As for you, if you walk before Me as your father David walked, even to do according to all that I have commanded you, and will keep My statutes and My ordinances, then I will establish your royal throne as I covenanted with your father David, saying, 'You shall not lack a man to be ruler in Israel. But if you turn away and forsake My statutes and My commandments which I have set before you, and go and serve other gods and worship them, then I will uproot you from My land which I have given you, and this house which I have consecrated for My name I will cast out of My sight and I will make it a proverb and a byword among all peoples. As for this house, which was exalted, everyone who passes by it will be astonished and say, Why has the Lord done thus to this land and to this house?' And they will say, 'Because they forsook the Lord, the God of their fathers who brought them from the land of Egypt, and they adopted other gods and worshiped them and served them; therefore He has brought all this adversity on them.'"

What God asks of Solomon is what He asks of us: walk according to His commandments. Unfortunately, many people do not know what God asks of us. We will only find this out by reading His Word and letting Him speak to us. God was very clear with Solomon that for the beautiful temple to stand and for David's descendants to sit on the throne, Solomon would have to follow God alone and forsake any false gods and idols. God wanted to bless Solomon's life and yet we see how easy it is to slowly drift away from our first love of Him. If it happened to Solomon, it can happen to any of us. We have to be diligent to stay in His Word, make sure we are in church learning about Him, and staying on track. If we don't, the consequences will always be devastating.

1 Kings 11:1-11, "Now King Solomon loved many foreign women along with the daughter of Pharaoh: Moabite, Ammonite, Edomite, Sidonian, and Hittite women, from the nations concerning which the Lord had said to the sons of Israel, 'You shall not associate with them, nor shall they associate with you, for they will surely turn your heart away after their gods.' Solomon held fast to these in love. He had seven hundred wives, princesses, and three hundred concubines, and his wives turned his heart away. For when Solomon was old, his wives turned his heart away after other gods; and his heart was not wholly devoted to the Lord his God, as the heart of David his father had been. For Solomon went after Ashtoreth the goddess of the Sidonians and after Milcom the detestable idol of the Ammonites. Solomon did what was evil in the sight of the Lord, and did not follow the Lord fully, as David his father had done. Then Solomon built a high place for Chemosh the detestable idol of Moab, on the mountain which is east of Jerusalem, and for Molech the detestable idol of the sons of Ammon. Thus also he did for all his foreign wives, who burned incense and sacrificed to their gods. Now the Lord was angry with Solomon because his heart was turned away from the Lord, the God of Israel, who had appeared to him twice, and had commanded him concerning this thing, that he should not go after other gods; but he did not observe what the Lord had commanded. So the Lord said to Solomon, 'Because you have done this, and you have not kept My covenant and My statutes, which I have commanded you, I will surely tear the kingdom from you, and will give it to your servant.'"

For Solomon, the consequences did not only affect himself but his children and the entire nation of Israel. There is always a cost to walking away from God and living in sin. If we can learn to connect this dot in our lives, think of the heartache we will save ourselves from. God gives His commands to us for our protection. Just like with Solomon, He wants us to live blessed, peaceful lives and the only way that can happen is to follow Him and obey His commands. Just like a parent wanting the best for his children, God also wants the best for us.

God is Faithful • • •

Now back to the saga of Abraham and Sarah taking matters into their own hands. The dot we want to connect is that regardless of Abraham and Sarah's sin, God was faithful to give him the son He promised.

Genesis 21:1-8, "Then the Lord took note of Sarai as He had said, and the Lord did for Sarah as He had promised. So Sarai conceived and bore a son to Abraham in his old age, at the appointed time of which God had spoken to him. Abraham called the name of his son who was born to him, whom Sarai bore to him, Isaac. Then Abraham circumcised his son Isaac when he was eight days old, as God had commanded him. Now Abraham was one hundred years old when his son Isaac was born to him. Sarai said, 'God has made laughter for me; everyone who hears will laugh with me.' And she said, 'Who would have said to Abraham that Sarai would nurse children? Yet I have borne him a son in his old age.' The child grew and was weaned, and Abraham made a great feast on the day that Isaac was weaned."

The descendants of Isaac flow all the way to Jesus – the promise to us for salvation. God will always remain faithful, even in the times of our lives when we are faithless. As a Christian, there is nothing we could ever do to thwart God's plan for us but in the process we have to recognize there are definite negative consequences to sin. That is why He wants us to wait on Him, which is incredibly difficult at times.

God is gracious and faithful and ready to forgive. He knows we are just people with sinful natures. That never, ever gives us an excuse to go out and sin, but it is comforting to know that those times when we do become selfish and walk away from God's best; He is there to pick us up and restore us.

Psalm 86:4-5, "Make glad the soul of Your servant, for to You, O Lord, I lift up my soul. For You, Lord, are good, and ready to forgive, and abundant in lovingkindness to all who call upon You."

Simon Peter is a great example of God's love and forgiveness. Simon was convinced he would never walk away from Jesus and yet when fear and dread came upon him; he did exactly what Jesus said he would do; deny Him.

Luke 22:31-34, "Simon, Simon, behold, Satan has demanded permission to sift you like wheat; but I have prayed for you, that your faith may not fail; and you, when once you have turned again, strengthen your brothers. But he said to Him, 'Lord, with You I am ready to go both to prison and to death!' And He said, 'I say to you, Peter, the rooster will not crow today until you have denied three times that you know Me.'"

After Jesus was crucified, buried and resurrected, this is what happened next:

Mark 16:1-7, "When the Sabbath was over, Mary Magdalene, and Mary the mother of James, and Salome, bought spices, so that they might come and anoint Him. Very early on the first day of the week, they came to the tomb when the sun had risen. They were saying to one another, 'Who will roll away the stone for us from the entrance of the tomb?' Looking up, they saw that the stone had been rolled away, although it was extremely large. Entering the tomb, they saw a young man sitting at the right, wearing a white robe; and they were amazed. And he said to

them, 'Do not be amazed; you are looking for Jesus the Nazarene, who has been crucified. He has risen; He is not here; behold, here is the place where they laid Him. <u>But go, tell His disciples and Peter,</u> He is going ahead of you to Galilee; there you will see Him, just as He told you.'" (underline our emphasis)

In spite of the wayward times in our lives, God is always faithful. The great part in this passage is that Jesus specifically singles out Peter and wants him to know He isn't upset with him. He wanted Peter to know that after the resurrection, even though he denied Him three times; God would and could still use him. We do not have to be paralyzed by our failures; God can still use us to serve Him.

We have a man at our church who got married. Through a series of unhealthy choices, he had an affair. His wife left him and they were divorced but the great thing about this story is that God was not done with this couple. Through a series of good choices, God brought these two back together and they were remarried. They now have a great ministry to others who are struggling with marriage and because of the bad choices that were made; they are able to help others. Failure never means God cannot still use us.

That is why it is so important to read our Bible; because in it is where we will find the great men of the Bible are just like us. Because we see how Abraham, Peter, Solomon and Sarai dealt with life, it gives us hope on how we should live our lives. They give us hope to know that God can still use us even when we fail.

Abraham and Sarai's failure was refusing to wait on God and yet in spite of their sin – God came through for them on His timing. This is a really important dot to connect – God's timing is not usually ours. When we realize this, we can wait with patience and confidence, knowing His way is better than ours. Sarah and Abraham had to deal with an immense amount of hurt in their lives, because they took matters into their own hands.

In spite of their failure to wait, God kept His promise to give Abraham a child.

Genesis 21:1-3, "Then the Lord took note of Sarai as He had said, and the Lord did for Sarai as He had promised. So Sarai conceived and bore a son to Abraham in his old age, at the appointed time of which God had spoken to him. Abraham called the name of his son who was born to him, whom Sarai bore to him, Isaac."

Many times God seems to be late for the things we need and yet He is always on time according to His schedule. He has purposes in allowing us to wait and for us; He is always trying to teach us to trust Him and not ourselves.

Because the economy is so unstable, at the time we are writing this, our financial situation seems to keep getting worse. Since the bank has barred the door from allowing us to get to our account that has money we need to live on, the problem has now become – where do we get money to make our payments? As difficult as this has become – we are learning daily what it truly means to trust Him to provide for us. We are also realizing there is a big difference between our wants and our needs. We "want" to re-stain our floors and go to Disneyland but we "need" to save our money and keep our business going. Since life is constantly changing – so does our wants and our needs and sometimes the most difficult part is recognizing there is a difference.

We have land for sale and someone has looked at it four times with the intent to purchase it. This man was on his way down, for a fifth time, to put something together and as he was leaving, his mother broke her hip and the trip had to be cancelled. We were so excited to sell this land since it would give us money to pay our bills and yet by God making us wait – we have actually learned how faithful He is to take care of us. Our youngest son had to go to the dentist and we weren't sure how we would pay the bill and the girl at the front said they were charging only the deductible because they wanted to bless us. The next week another son had a serious issue that required more money down than we knew we had and yet when we put what little cash we had with a credit card we were able to pay the bill. Somehow, God always comes through and yet, just like Abraham and Sarah, He usually calls us to wait so we can see what HE will do and then HE gets all the credit!

Life is filled with twists and turns. For Abraham and Sarah, the same was true for them. They were promised a child in their old age. They refused to believe God could make this happen so they took matters into their own hands. They had to pay an enormous consequence as Sarah was jealous of Abraham's child by Hagar. In the end, after Sarah got her baby of promise, the heartache for Abraham still continued as Sarah forced her husband to drive Hagar and Ishmael out of their lives. The result of their refusal to wait on God and the demand of Sarah "distressed Abraham greatly" since he loved his son Ishmael who was now approximately 17 years old.

Genesis 21:9-14, "Now Sarah saw the son of Hagar the Egyptian, whom she had borne to Abraham, mocking. Therefore she said to Abraham, 'Drive out this maid and her son, for the son of this maid shall not be an heir with my son Isaac.' The matter distressed Abraham greatly because of his son. But God said to Abraham, 'Do not be distressed because of the lad and your maid; whatever Sarah tells you, listen to her, for through Isaac your descendants shall be named. And of the son of the maid I will make a nation also, because he is your descendant.' So Abraham rose early in the morning and took bread and a skin of water and gave them to Hagar, putting them on her shoulder, and gave her the boy, and sent her away. And she departed and wandered about in the wilderness of Beersheba."

Connecting this dot in our lives is key to living a peaceful life...wait. Wait on God. Wait for His peace. Wait for His timing. What we learn from the story of Abraham and Sarah is that when we refuse to wait on Him – the effects can be devastating. Wait for God's best for you to marry. Wait for the job you are certain He has given you. Wait on God before you walk out on your marriage. Wait.

When God is ready for you to make a move and when the timing is right – you will have a peace beyond measure. You will know in your heart and in your mind that God is in the decisions you are making. Read your Bible. Wait for Him to speak to you through His Word and through the counsel of godly men and women in your life along with the changes in your circumstances. Abraham and Sarah could have by-passed many hurtful emotions and actions if they had just connected this dot of waiting on God.

Psalm 29:11, "The Lord will give strength to His people; The Lord will bless His people with peace."

Psalm 85:8, "I will hear what God the Lord will say; for He will speak peace to His people, to His godly ones; but let them not turn back to folly."

Psalm 119:165, "Those who love Your law have great peace, and nothing causes them to stumble."

Dots to Connect

- God's timing is usually different from ours.

- God always has a purpose behind our waiting.

- Sometimes it takes trials and tribulations to show us that God is really in charge of everything.

- When we are put in difficult situations our only option is to cry out to the Lord, which is exactly where He wants us – trusting Him!

- God wants us to refuse to be fearful, wait on Him, and recognize He will accomplish what we need since we know He is fighting for us.

- When God seems silent – He is only building our faith and teaching us to trust Him and not ourselves.

- God is always working behind the scenes to make things happen in His perfect time.

- We must be careful not to rationalize and start taking matters into our own hands.

- In spite of our failures, God is always faithful.

- God calls us to wait on Him so we can see what He does for His glory!

- You will have peace, beyond measure, when you wait on the Lord for His perfect timing.

Chapter 8

Set Apart for God

When God called Abraham out of Ur, He promised him a nation would be built through him. Twenty-five years after God told Abraham this, Sarah finally was pregnant and in this child, the nation of Israel would be born.

Genesis 17:1-8, "Now when Abram was ninety-nine years old, the Lord appeared to Abram and said to him, 'I am God Almighty; walk before Me, and be blameless. I will establish My covenant between Me and you, and I will multiply you exceedingly.' Abram fell on his face, and God talked with him, saying, 'As for Me, behold, My covenant is with you, and you will be the father of a multitude of nations. No longer shall your name be called Abram, but your name shall be Abraham; for I will make you the father of a multitude of nations. I have made you exceedingly fruitful, and I will make nations of you, and kings will come forth from you. I will establish My covenant between Me and you and your descendants after you throughout their generations for an everlasting covenant, to be God to you and to your descendants after you. I will give to you and to your descendants after you, the land of your sojournings, all the land of Canaan, for an everlasting possession; and I will be their God.'"

God was making a promise to Abraham that he would have many descendants, he would be the father of many nations and the land of Canaan (modern day Israel) would be His people. The amazing thing is that over 4,000 years later, the tiny nation of Israel still exists. Why would such a small and insignificant piece of land be so important to the world? Why is the world fixated on the problems in the Middle East where Israel is the center of attention? Because God made a promise thousands of years ago that this land was for his people, the Jewish nation. Because the Israelites (modern day Jews) were a people from God, they needed something that would set them apart from others. God wanted them to make a covenant back to Him in the form of circumcision.

Genesis 17:9-12 God said further to Abraham, **"Now as for you, you shall keep My covenant, you and your descendants after you throughout their generations. This is My covenant, which you shall keep, between Me and you and your descendants after you: every male among you shall be circumcised. And you shall be circumcised in the flesh of your foreskin, and it shall be the sign of the covenant between Me and you. And every male among you who is eight days old shall be circumcised throughout your generations, a servant who is born in the house or who is bought with money from any foreigner, who is not of your descendants."**

Dr. Ray Pritchard in his sermon on this passage says:

"Why pick something like circumcision? I think the answer goes something like this. Circumcision by its nature touches the very core of what it meant to be a man. In his most intimate and personal moment each Jewish male would forever be reminded that he was a holy Son of the Covenant and that he belonged to God. No one else might know it but once he was circumcised, he could never forget it."

Circumcision was a sign, in the Old Testament, that a person belonged to God. The New Testament initiates baptism as a sign that we belong to God. God commanded circumcision, in the Old

Testament, and Jesus commanded baptism, in the New Testament. Just like circumcision and baptism, so should our lives be an outward sign to others that we are believers.

The dot we want to connect is that when a person accepts Christ into their life, they become a new person and because of this their lives will look different.

2 Corinthians 5:17 says, "Therefore if anyone is in Christ, he is a new creature; the old things passed away; behold, new things have come."

Becoming a devoted follower of Jesus means our lives will change. We will have new motives in life, new desires, new actions and new attitudes. Just like circumcision was a sign, so our new lives in Christ will be a sign.

Colossians 3:5-13, "Therefore consider the members of your earthly body as dead to immorality, impurity, passion, evil desire, and greed, which amounts to idolatry. For it is because of these things that the wrath of God will come upon the sons of disobedience, and in them you also once walked, when you were living in them. But now you also, put them all aside: anger, wrath, malice, slander, and abusive speech from your mouth. Do not lie to one another, since you laid aside the old self with its evil practices, and have put on the new self who is being renewed to a true knowledge according to the image of the One who created him— a renewal in which there is no distinction between Greek and Jew, circumcised and uncircumcised, barbarian, Scythian, slave and freeman, but Christ is all, and in all. So, as those who have been chosen of God, holy and beloved, put on a heart of compassion, kindness, humility, gentleness and patience; bearing with one another, and forgiving each other, whoever has a complaint against anyone; just as the Lord forgave you, so also should you."

The Bible also says our lives will be seen by others as a light. If you think about a light – it pierces the darkness. For example, in the midst of anger, wrath, malice and slander – we as Christians are to have compassion, kindness gentleness and patience. One is darkness and the other is light. We are called as Christians to be the light to a very dark world.

Matthew 5:14-16, "You are the light of the world. A city set on a hill cannot be hidden; nor does anyone light a lamp and put it under a basket, but on the lampstand, and it gives light to all who are in the house. Let your light shine before men in such a way that they may see your good works, and glorify your Father who is in heaven."

When we decide to follow Christ, we need to know that God calls us to be different. We have to be set apart from the rest of the world. Our non-Christian neighbors need to see us get up and go to church. They need to see we are friendly and helpful and care about others. People are watching us at our workplace to see if the faith we claim affects our actions. Do we gossip? Do we steal? Do we work more diligently than others? Being a Christian entails serving others. Are we involved in ministries where we are giving our lives away? What about serving the poor, working with the homeless or helping people in our neighborhoods who are in need?

Jesus says, in the verse above, that we are to be lights in the world and when we care about others and show the love of Christ, people will take notice. As they see our lives, they will want to know why. Why do we **not** panic when the economy is failing? Why do we **refuse** to fall apart when there is a terrorist attack? Why are we **not** fearful of death? Why do we have a peace in life that others do not?

All of these attitudes are attributed to the fact we belong to God. We have been set apart to serve Him and the people around us should feel the benefits of a life lived for Christ. The Bible makes it clear that we have to be different; not in a weird way but in a good way. Being "set apart" for God entails a few things:

- If we say we are Christians and yet walk in a continual pattern of sin, the Bible makes it clear we might not understand what it means to be a Christian. **1 John 1:6-8** states, **"If we say that we have fellowship with Him and yet walk in the darkness, we lie and do not practice the truth; but if we walk in the Light as He Himself is in the Light, we have fellowship with one another, and the blood of Jesus His Son cleanses us from all sin. If we say that we have no sin, we are deceiving ourselves and the truth is not in us."** As a Christian, when we are living in continual patterns of sin without any remorse or repentance, we need to check ourselves to see if we are truly in the faith. When we say we are believers our actions must reflect our words. We need to remember that we all sin – even Christians, but a true Christian has a heartfelt sadness and brokenness over his sin.

- The Bible makes it clear that if we truly know Him we will keep His commandments. **1 John 2:3-6** says, **"By this we know that we have come to know Him, if we keep His commandments. The one who says, 'I have come to know Him,' and does not keep His commandments, is a liar, and the truth is not in him; but whoever keeps His word, in him the love of God has truly been perfected. By this we know that we are in Him: the one who says he abides in Him ought himself to walk in the same manner as He walked."**

We were talking with some people today, who were new believers, and they were so fearful they were not following all the rules of being a Christian. Most people assume that being a Christian is a set of "don't do this" or "you can't do that" kind of rules. We tried to explain to them that God's rules were set up to protect us – not to harm us.

Adultery causes a loss of trust and the breakup of marriages.
Pre-marital sex causes unwanted pregnancy and heartache.
Drugs and alcohol can cause addictions which destroys families.
Murder puts people in prison for a lifetime.
Stealing can cause a loss of trust.
Anger can cause physical abuse.
Shady business deals can destroy a company.

God does not give us rules so we can't have any fun – He gives us commandments that help us make it through life with integrity and wisdom. He loves us and wants what is best for us and He knows how harmful sin can be to us and those around us. When we are Christians, we obey His commands through the power of the Holy Spirit because we love and trust Him, knowing He has our best interests at heart.

- The Bible makes it clear that as Christians we will love people. That means we will love the people who are easy to love as well as the people who are difficult to love. Just like we have already learned, Jesus calls us to be different and pray for those who hurt us or use us. **John 2:9-11, "The one who says he is in the Light and yet hates his brother is in the darkness until now. The one who loves his brother abides in the Light and there is no cause for stumbling in him. But the one who hates his brother is in the darkness and walks in the darkness, and does not know where he is going because the darkness has blinded his eyes."**

- As Christians we are called to practice righteousness. When we become Christians, the Holy Spirit lives inside of us and He moves us to do the right things. Have you ever watched a movie that a year ago didn't bother you but suddenly the words and the actions appall you? Have you ever caught yourself gossiping and realized how wrong it felt? Have you ever gotten angry at someone and yet realized it was only because of your own selfishness that you were upset? All of these scenarios show a growth pattern in our walk with Jesus. As He is living in us, He is moving us away from unrighteous living and moving us to a life a practicing righteousness. **1 John 3:7-10, "Little children, make sure no one deceives you; the one who practices righteousness is righteous, just as He is righteous; the one who practices sin is of the devil; for the devil has sinned from the beginning. The Son of God appeared for this purpose, to destroy the works of the devil. No one who is born of God practices sin, because His seed abides in him; and he cannot sin, because he is born of God. By this the children of God and the children of the devil are obvious: anyone who does not practice righteousness is not of God, nor the one who does not love his brother.**

The dot we are trying to connect is that our actions must show others our faith. Abraham had the covenant of circumcision which was an outward sign that he was set apart for God. Our lives must be lived in such a way as an outward sign that nonbelievers can see there is a difference. Our lives should produce, for others to see, attributes like:

Hope
  Faith
    Peace
      Patience
        Joy
          Love
            Kindness
              Gentleness

Galatians 5:22-25, "But the fruit of the Spirit is love, joy, peace, patience, kindness, goodness, faithfulness, gentleness, self-control; against such things there is no law. Now those who belong to Christ Jesus have crucified the flesh with its passions and desires. If we live by the Spirit, let us also walk by the Spirit."

We should be the people who are the most **encouraging**. A few weeks ago, I (Rob) was a little discouraged when I got a phone call from someone I hadn't heard from in months. He called just to tell me I had been on his mind and he just wanted to let me know things would be okay. We all need to be encouraged – we need to call someone when we know they are struggling. Sometimes just hearing someone say "it will be okay" is just what we need to hear for the moment.

We should be the **kindest** people around. I (Lisa) was pulling out of our house the other day and before I got to our dirt road a car pulled in front of me. This back road is dirt and when a car is in front of us, we drive for miles with dirt on our windshield. I noticed, as the lady pulled in front of me, that she had a Christian sticker on her back window. Just before I could get annoyed, she pulled over and let me pass her. Evidently, she had not seen me and when she did, she felt bad for pulling in front of me. It was one of those moments where I got to see a Christian truly living out her faith. I wanted to stop and tell her how much I appreciated what she did – she was living out kindness.

We should be the most **peaceful, hopeful** people around. When circumstances seem to overwhelm us, we should be the ones who are not stressed or worried. We need to show people around us that we trust the God we serve to take care of us – we need to show people that when we get sick or hurt or when life gives us a bad turn – we are the ones who are peaceful and hopeful knowing that all things – good and bad – will be used by God to get us where we need to be. We have a friend who is a pastor and his daughter was in a very serious car accident. When he was at the hospital, the nurses were shocked at the way he was handling the stress about his daughter. He had a peace about him because he knew God. He understood God had a plan for his daughter's life, and wanted others to understand what it means to trust a God that is in control of everything.

We should be the most **loving** people around. We should care for those who are hurting, we should pray for someone instead of gossip, and we should help those in need. As a Christian we recognize our lives need to be about others and not ourselves; that could mean loving a family member, spouse, friend, neighbor or coworker. We need to be the ones people come to when they are hurting because they see we truly care about others.

We should be the most **patient** and **gentle** people around. We hear the phrase "it's not what you say but it is how you say it that is the problem" which makes sense. But, as believers, we should be the ones who refuse to get angry. If we need to talk or confront someone it should always be with a spirit of gentleness. We have to remember that people are human and have bad days. We need to be patient. We need to keep in mind that as Christians, how we talk is truly important. We can scream and yell at our children or we can be gentle. We can get frustrated with people and circumstances or we can be patient.

This is why our actions really do matter. The reason many people refuse to follow Jesus is because the hypocrisy between our faith and how we act. The Bible is clear, when we tell others we are Christians or they see us going to church, they expect us to act differently. These verses that follow show us how different we need to be acting in order to testify our lives have been changed by a relationship with Christ.

1 Corinthians 1:4-6, "I thank my God always concerning you for the grace of God which was given you in Christ Jesus, that in everything you were enriched in Him, in all speech and all knowledge, even as the testimony concerning Christ was confirmed in you."

Colossians 3:8-10, "But now you also, put them all aside: anger, wrath, malice, slander, and abusive speech from your mouth. Do not lie to one another, since you laid aside the old self with its evil practices, and have put on the new self who is being renewed to

a true knowledge according to the image of the One who created him."

Colossians 4:6, "Let your speech always be with grace, as though seasoned with salt, so that you will know how you should respond to each person."

1 Timothy 4:12, "Let no one look down on your youthfulness, but rather in speech, conduct, love, faith and purity, show yourself an example of those who believe."

As Christians, shouldn't these things look different in our lives?

- *Shouldn't we have knowledge about God?*
- *Shouldn't we put aside anger, wrath, malice, slander and abusive speech?*
- *Shouldn't we refuse to lie?*
- *Shouldn't we be the one's speaking with grace?*
- *Shouldn't our speech, conduct, love, faith and purity shows others our faith?*

This dot ***must*** be connected if we are ever to have an impact on this world for Jesus. When we come to Christ it must be with a heart of belief, repentance and faith. Many people are great about the belief and faith part but they do not want anything to do with the repentance part. When a person truly comes to Christ, **Ezekiel 36: 26-27** promises **"Moreover, I will give you a new heart and put a new spirit within you; and I will remove the heart of stone from your flesh and give you a heart of flesh. I will put My Spirit within you and cause you to walk in My statutes, and you will be careful to observe My ordinances."**

Repenting means to turn around and go the other way. This is where the Word of God and the Spirit of God works in our lives. As we read our Bibles, we will begin to see attitudes and actions that need to be changed and the Spirit of God will convict us and help us. He will give us the ability to walk away from destructive lifestyles. Being a Christian will be marked by our repentant heart.

Matthew 3:2, "Repent, for the kingdom of heaven is at hand."

Matthew 3:8, "Therefore bear fruit in keeping with repentance."

Matthew 4:17, "From that time Jesus began to preach and say, 'Repent, for the kingdom of heaven is at hand.'"

Matthew 11:2, "Now when John, while imprisoned, heard of the works of Christ, he sent word by his disciples."

Mark 1:4, "John the Baptist appeared in the wilderness preaching a baptism of repentance for the forgiveness of sins."

Mark 1:15, "The time is fulfilled, and the kingdom of God is at hand; repent and believe in the gospel."

Mark 6:12, "They went out and preached that men should repent."

Luke 5:32, "I have not come to call the righteous but sinners to repentance."

Luke 15:7, "I tell you that in the same way, there will be more joy in heaven over one sinner who repents than over ninety-nine righteous persons who need no repentance."

2 Corinthians 7:9-10, "I now rejoice, not that you were made sorrowful, but that you were made sorrowful to the point of repentance; for you were made sorrowful according to the will of God, so that you might not suffer loss in anything through us. For the sorrow that is according to the will of God produces a repentance without regret, leading to salvation, but the sorrow of the world produces death."

Revelation 2:10, "Do not fear what you are about to suffer. Behold, the devil is about to cast some of you into prison, so that you will be tested, and you will have tribulation for ten days. Be faithful until death, and I will give you the crown of life."

As we grow in our relationship with Christ, we will notice from one year to the next how our attitudes and actions are changing. Here are some things He may want to change in our lives so we will have a greater impact on the world for Jesus. When we are living in any of these lifestyles and claiming Christ, we will fall into the "hypocrite" category and will have no impact on this world. These are just a few things He clearly calls us in His Word to repent from.

Adultery – Fornication – Homosexuality - Jealousy – Anger – Quarreling – Gossip - Lying - Cheating - Hurting others

Galatians 5:19-21, "Now the deeds of the flesh are evident, which are: immorality, impurity, sensuality, idolatry, sorcery, enmities, strife, jealousy, outbursts of anger, disputes, dissensions, factions, envying, drunkenness, carousing, and things like these, of which I forewarn you, just as I have forewarned you, that those who practice such things will not inherit the kingdom of God."

1 Corinthians 6:9-11, "Or do you not know that the unrighteous will not inherit the kingdom of God? Do not be deceived; neither fornicators, nor idolaters, nor adulterers, nor effeminate, nor homosexuals, nor thieves, nor the covetous, nor drunkards, nor revilers, nor swindlers, will inherit the kingdom of God. Such were some of you; but you were washed, but you were sanctified, but you were justified in the name of the Lord Jesus Christ and in the Spirit of our God."

Why would these things be important to God? What does it matter if I am living with my girlfriend? Who cares if we are having sex before we get married? Why should anyone care that I am having an affair since I am unhappy at home? What's the big deal if I go to parties and get drunk? Will God condemn me if I am a homosexual? Didn't He make me this way?

The Bible deals with all of these issues. Sin brings on heartache and destruction and as His children, He wants us to avoid both. We are to be witnesses for Him. We are to be the ones who share Him with others and yet, when our lives are filled with unhealthy, ungodly, and unholy attitudes and actions – we have no affect on people. Our purpose for our lives as Christians is found in **Matthew 28:19-20, "Go therefore and make disciples of all the nations, baptizing them in the name of the Father and the Son and the Holy Spirit, teaching them to observe all that I commanded you; and lo, I am with you always, even to the end of the age."**

This is what we sign up for when we become a Christian. We have a job to share Christ and teach others what He has commanded us. If we are living in a sinful lifestyle, then our job of working for God means nothing. We have no impact. People may have a difficult time coming to Christ. In **1 Corinthians 6** on the previous page, Paul tells the Corinthian church that the people who are practicing these sinful actions and lifestyles will not inherit the Kingdom of God. He makes it clear that a person could live like this until they become Christians and then their lives change. Paul says **"and such were some of you…"** We could come from any one of these lifestyles and yet when Jesus comes in our lives – He transforms us and changes us so we can be an influence on others.

In Abraham's day the sign of circumcision was a sign they belonged to God. What we are hoping for, in this chapter, is making sure our lives are a sign to others. Not a sign hidden behind a tree or a sign that is blank – but a sign showing others our faith is real. Jesus is real. He lives in us and He transforms our lives and our character. We need to be walking billboards for Jesus and by our lives, show others what it means to be set apart for God and a truly devoted follower of His.

Romans 2:28-29, "For he is not a Jew who is one outwardly, nor is circumcision that which is outward in the flesh. But he is a Jew who is one inwardly; and circumcision is that which is of the heart, by the Spirit, not by the letter; and his praise is not from men, but from God."

Dots to Connect

- Our lives must be lived in such a way that others will see we are Christians by our actions. Our lives are the best testimony.

- When we come to Christ we will have new motives, new desires, new actions, and new attitudes.

- God calls us to be "set apart" and our faith must be seen by others through our words and actions.

- We cannot say we are Christians and yet live in a continual pattern of sin.

- The Bible says, if we truly know Him, we will keep His commandments.

- God gives us commandments to help us make it through life with integrity and wisdom.

- As Christians we will love people.

- As Christians we will practice righteousness.

- We should be the most encouraging, kindest, peaceful, hopeful, loving, patient and gentle people around.

- We will not have an impact for Christ if we live in an unrepentant lifestyle of sin.

Chapter 9

Finally..!

Twenty five years is a long time to wait for anything. For Sarai – the waiting for a baby was over in her mind; she was ninety years old and Abraham was one hundred. Babies were unheard of at that age. She was probably tired of hearing the promises God was making since she had moved to the Promised Land twenty-five years earlier. In her mind, she most likely thought God had forgotten her. She was old and Abraham already had a son by her maid who was now around fourteen years old. She loved Abraham and desperately wanted a child but time slipped away and now it was too late. The promise never came through and in her mind it probably never would.

Do you ever feel that way? Do you ever think it is too late and God cannot possibly come through? Maybe it is a loveless marriage, a sickness, a financial burden or a prayer you have been praying for years. It feels over; it is clearly too late. It would make sense Sarai felt that way too. For years she struggled with barrenness and watched her husband grow to love a son that was not hers. We can feel the tension and the struggle she must have gone through every day of her life as she woke up knowing the biological clock was past midnight and the God she believed would answer her prayer was not doing what He said He would.

For many in these situations – they walk away from God. They decided a long time ago when their prayers were not answered in the manner they were praying – God must not be real. He must not care or He would have come through for them. Heartache turned to cynicism and for Sarai – she possibly felt the same way. Then, clear out of the blue – three visitors show up and give her some unbelievable news.

Genesis 18:1-9, "Now the Lord appeared to him by the oaks of Mamre, while he was sitting at the tent door in the heat of the day. When he lifted up his eyes and looked, behold, three men were standing opposite him; and when he saw them, he ran from the tent door to meet them and bowed himself to the earth, and said, 'My Lord, if now I have found favor in Your sight, please do not pass Your servant by. Please let a little water be brought and wash your feet, and rest yourselves under the tree; and I will bring a piece of bread, that you may refresh yourselves; after that you may go on, since you have visited your servant.' And they said, 'So do, as you have said.' So Abraham hurried into the tent to Sarai, and said, 'Quickly, prepare three measures of fine flour, knead it and make bread cakes.' Abraham also ran to the herd, and took a tender and choice calf and gave it to the servant, and he hurried to prepare it. He took curds and milk and the calf which he had prepared, and placed it before them; and he was standing by them under the tree as they ate. Then they said to him, 'Where is Sarai your wife?' And he said, 'There, in the tent.'"

It was just another hot, miserable summer day for Abraham and Sarai when these visitors arrived with some news that would change the course of history and would also change the cynicism toward God she probably had been feeling. In one moment – the news she had wanted to hear for twenty five years was being announced and as she was eavesdropping on the conversation – she couldn't believe what she was hearing! A baby? At her age? Needless to say – she laughed!

Genesis 18:10-15, "He said, 'I will surely return to you at this time next year; and behold, Sarai your wife will have a son.' And Sarai was listening at the tent door, which was behind him. Now Abraham and Sarai were old, advanced in age; Sarai was past childbearing. Sarai laughed to herself, saying, 'After I have become old, shall I have pleasure, my lord being old also?' And the Lord said to Abraham, 'Why did Sarai laugh, saying, Shall I indeed bear a child, when I am so old? Is anything too difficult for the Lord? At the appointed time I will return to you, at this time next year, and Sarai will have a son.' Sarai denied it however, saying, 'I did not laugh'; for she was afraid. And He said, 'No, but you did laugh.'"

We wonder what kind of laugh it was. Could it be she thought this was a funny joke and laughed? Maybe it was laugh that covered the disbelief and heartache she felt for all these years. Maybe it was a fearful laugh that exposed her fear of being let down once again. Haven't we all been at that same place? Maybe you prayed for years that God would do something and, like Sarai, twenty five years you are still waiting.

Maybe we would laugh like Sarai if someone came and told us after twenty five years of praying and waiting that:

Our drug addicted child would return home…
    Our cancer would be healed…
        We would feel love for our spouse again…
            Our relatives would come to Christ…
            Our addiction would finally go away…

Would we laugh? Would we be so tired and cynical over years of seemingly unanswered prayers that we chuckle in our hearts; never truly believing God would or could come through?

For Sarai, she can't seem to believe God could do something so incredibly impossible. Yes, He is God. Yes, she believes in Him.

But trust Him? Probably not. For Sarai she was probably thinking:

"You told me, God, I would have a baby and I don't."

"I thought I was doing the right thing, God, by giving Hagar to my husband but my life has been wrought with sadness and heartache watching him love another woman's child."

"I waited for years and years for you, God, to come through and yet each month left me more disappointed than before."

Haven't we all felt that in some way? Isn't it easy to be cynical about God when He keeps us waiting? Isn't it easy to quit trusting Him and start to trust ourselves? The problem is that when we stop trusting Him, more than likely we will stop growing in our faith and then it snowballs down from there. We start rationalizing that if God really cared about us He would have done something sooner. Since He seems distant and uncaring, we grow farther and farther from Him and it all started because we did not like His timing. We start to forget He loves us more than we can imagine. We forget He cares for us more than we care for ourselves. Then we forget He has a perfect plan for our lives that sometimes includes not getting what we think we want, when we want it.

For Sarai , God had so much to teach her as she was waiting for a child. God was teaching her how important it was to refuse to run ahead of Him. He was teaching her how to love those that were unlovable. She had to learn to forgive her husband and forgive herself. All of this was part of God's plan for her life and we have to recognize He has a plan for our lives as well.

The same is true for those of us who are still waiting for God to show up. He is using this time to show us that He is the One who controls everything. He controls the job we are looking for, the baby we so desperately want and the spouse we want to change. He is the change agent for our wayward children or the person who hurt us deeply. *It all has to come back to God, to know Him so well that trusting Him becomes part of who we are.*

Suddenly, just like Sarai, we begin to realize we cannot change our situation.

For us, we realize we cannot control the failing economy or bring success to our company. We work diligently to call on dentists but ultimately God moves on their hearts to buy our products. We recognize the woman in our life who is desperately trying to get pregnant will not do so until God opens her womb. We understand that our friend's children who seem to be walking away from God, at the moment, are completely under His hand and He has a journey for their lives that we might not be excited about, at the moment. We begin to grasp the fact that God alone changes hearts, changes circumstances and changes people. Nothing we say or do can override what God is doing.

When we get this, it will change our life.

Proverbs 21:1 says, "The king's heart is like channels of water in the hand of the Lord; He turns it wherever He wishes."

Finally, God steps in, on His timing and in His way, and Sarai gets pregnant against all odds. She and Abraham were both beyond child bearing years and yet God wanted to show them four thousand years ago and us four thousand years later that He can do anything. God had a nation to build and through Abraham and Sarai's child, this became a reality. Would Sarah have trusted God twenty five years earlier? Would she have given the credit to God alone for her child? Probably not and yet when she finally conceived, she knew it could only be God.

Genesis 21:1-7, "Then the Lord took note of Sarai as He had said, and the Lord did for Sarai as He had promised. So Sarai conceived and bore a son to Abraham in his old age, at the

appointed time of which God had spoken to him. Abraham called the name of his son who was born to him, whom Sarai bore to him, Isaac. Then Abraham circumcised his son Isaac when he was eight days old, as God had commanded him. Now Abraham was one hundred years old when his son Isaac was born to him. Sarai said, 'God has made laughter for me; everyone who hears will laugh with me.' And she said, 'Who would have said to Abraham that Sarai would nurse children? Yet I have borne him a son in his old age.'"

The dot we need to connect is this: God always has a purpose behind our waiting and it is usually to teach us to trust Him more. We need to recognize, just like Sarai, that we have a choice. We can be pessimistic and annoyed when we do not get our own way. We can be frustrated and mad when we do not get the answers we are looking for. Or, we can see the hand of God in EVERYTHING. When things turn bad, we lose a job, we get a disease, or we have problems in our marriage, we do not ever have to fall apart because we know the God who holds our life in His hand. Just like He had a purpose in making Sarai wait, He too has a purpose for making us wait in difficult situations. He has a purpose in everything that comes into our lives and when we begin to understand this, there is never a need for stress or worry. With each step, good or bad, we learn to trust Him knowing He is moving us to the place He wants us.

Just like Sarai, God wants us to know He alone is the giver of everything. He wants us to trust He has the best intentions and interests in mind to further His kingdom. Our lives cannot be about us – it has to be about Him. Only when we surrender to Him our entire lives; our family, children, home, and job can He do the work that needs to be done. That is what being a Christian is all about. Surrendering our wants and needs to Him and allowing Him to use us to advance the gospel. God had His plan for Abraham and Sarai just like He has a plan for us.

Dots to Connect

- God is involved even if our prayers are not answered in our time and in our way.

- We must be careful not to be cynical when we do not get the answers we want – we need to recognize God has a better plan.

- God always wants to teach us something while we are waiting.

- God is in control of the economy, our children, and our jobs...nothing we can say or do will ever over ride what He is doing.

- By waiting on God – we learn what it truly means to trust Him and then give Him all the credit for the outcome.

- We have a choice while waiting - we can become pessimistic and angry with God or we can relax and wait on Him as we choose to see His hand in everything.

Chapter 10

Our Faith and How We Affect Others

Abraham's nephew, Lot, gives us some sad examples of how easy it is to get caught up in sin and how that sin has an impact on others. When Abraham and Lot moved into the Promised Land, Lot lived under the protection of Abraham. As they split apart Lot moved near the city of Sodom and then eventually moved into the city and became a part of it. That is what happens as we move closer and closer to sin and sin usually seems fun to begin with. We start to rationalize, we start to like what sin does for us and then we become so affected by it that we have no witness any longer for Christ.

In Genesis 19 we see Lot sitting at the gate in Sodom. In the Old Testament, sitting at the city gate most likely meant you were someone of prominence in the city. **Proverbs 31:23** states, **"Her husband is known in the gates, when he sits among the elders of the land."** and **Genesis 34:20** says, **"So Hamor and his son Shechem came to the gate of their city and spoke to the men of their city, saying…"** We are not sure if Lot knew these two men coming into the city were angels but he did act very reverent to them and begged them to stay at his house.

Genesis 19:1-3, Now the two angels came to Sodom in the evening

as Lot was sitting in the gate of Sodom. When Lot saw them, he rose to meet them and bowed down with his face to the ground. And he said, "Now behold, my lords, please turn aside into your servant's house, and spend the night, and wash your feet; then you may rise early and go on your way." They said however, "No, but we shall spend the night in the square." Yet he urged them strongly, so they turned aside to him and entered his house; and he prepared a feast for them, and baked unleavened bread, and they ate.

Lot clearly knew how wicked the city of Sodom was and he was fearful for these two men who showed up. We can see from the next few verses how sick and disgusting this sin infested city had become.

Genesis 19:4-8, Before they lay down, the men of the city, the men of Sodom, surrounded the house, both young and old, all the people from every quarter; and they called to Lot and said to him, "Where are the men who came to you tonight? Bring them out to us that we may have relations with them." But Lot went out to them at the doorway, and shut the door behind him, and said, "Please, my brothers, do not act wickedly. "Now behold, I have two daughters who have not had relations with man; please let me bring them out to you, and do to them whatever you like; only do nothing to these men, inasmuch as they have come under the shelter of my roof."

Think of this scene. All the men of the city, young and old, from grade school to grandfathers all gathered to have a homosexual gang rape experience with these two men who unbeknownst to the town, were angels. If that isn't pathetic enough, Lot decides to hand over his virgin daughters to the men of this town to do whatever they wanted with them. That is how fast and far sin can move us. Lot has moved from the protection of Abraham, to the outskirts of the city, to living in the city to actually calling these evil, wicked men "my brothers."

That is how sin creeps into our lives and before we know it we are in Sodom with people who have no regard for the things of God. We begin to become just like them, compromising our standards and destroying any witness we have for the gospel. **James 1:14-16** shows us the downward spiral that begins with temptation, **"But each one is tempted when he is carried away and enticed by his own lust. Then when lust has conceived, it gives birth to sin; and when sin is accomplished, it brings forth death. Do not be deceived, my beloved brethren."**

Many people live in difficult situations. Maybe it is a job you go to where you are surrounded by wicked people all day long. Perhaps it is your home where your spouse or children want nothing to do with God. Possibly it is your school or your dorm where nobody wants anything to do with your Christian faith. We all have a choice: stand up for our faith or join in with the crowd moving toward Sodom.

Jesus calls us as Christians to be different, to be **in** the world but not **of** the world. We cannot live in a Christian comfort zone but instead we are called to go into our neighborhoods, workplace, home and school and be a light to those around us. Unfortunately for Lot, when he did try and take a stand, his family thought he was joking.

Genesis 19:9-14, But they said, "Stand aside." Furthermore, they said, "This one came in as an alien, and already he is acting like a judge; now we will treat you worse than them." So they pressed hard against Lot and came near to break the door. But the men reached out their hands and brought Lot into the house with them, and shut the door. They struck the men who were at the doorway of the house with blindness, both small and great, so that they wearied themselves trying to find the doorway. Then the two men said to Lot, "Whom else have you here? A son-in-law, and your sons, and your daughters, and whomever you have in the city, bring them out of the place; for we are about to destroy this place, because their outcry has become so great

before the Lord that the Lord has sent us to destroy it." Lot went out and spoke to his sons-in-law, who were to marry his daughters, and said, "Up, get out of this place, for the Lord will destroy the city." But he appeared to his sons-in-law to be jesting.

This is one of those heartbreaking scenes in the Bible where we see how our lives truly affect other people. Lot knew God and yet instead of living for God and trying to point people to a relationship with Him, he evidently didn't live out his faith. It was so bad that when Lot told his son-in-laws to run because the Lord would destroy the city, they thought he was joking.

Now let's look at our own lives. What do people think about our faith? Are we living out what we believe so if we talked about our relationship with Christ others wouldn't think we were joking? What if we asked them to church? What if we told them we read our Bibles? What if we gave them Biblical counsel? Do our lives look more like a true believer or do we look more like Lot? Have we become so like the world and those around us that our light for Christ has been dimmed?

Matthew 5:14-16, "You are the light of the world. A city set on a hill cannot be hidden; nor does anyone light a lamp and put it under a basket, but on the lampstand, and it gives light to all who are in the house. "Let your light shine before men in such a way that they may see your good works, and glorify your Father who is in heaven."

Lukewarm Christians • • •

When we become Christians, we do so under the pretense of surrender. Jesus died on the cross for us and gave His life so we in turn could spend eternity with Him. In our culture, we think that is where it ends. We need to know what true, Biblical Christianity is all about and it begins and ends with surrendering our lives to Christ and to live for Him on a daily basis.

In the book of Revelation, Jesus is speaking to John regarding seven churches that have lost their way since He was resurrected. He is having John write letters to these churches to show them what they are doing right and what they are doing wrong. In Revelation 3, John is told to write a letter to the church of Laodicea because they were lukewarm in the way they lived their Christian lives. They claimed to know Christ but their lives never stood out as followers of Him. These people showed up at church, threw some money in the offering plate and then went about their daily lives as if Jesus were not a part of it.

Jesus hates us to live a lukewarm Christian life. He says in Revelation 3:16, **"So because you are lukewarm, and neither hot nor cold, I will spit you out of My mouth."** Jesus wants us to be on fire for Him because when we are, we have an impact for Him in this world. When Lot decided to speak up for God and his son-in-laws thought he was joking – that is a sad commentary on how sin had so devastated his life and witness that even his family refused to believe him. Hopefully, this will challenge us to look at our own lives to see if we are affecting our families, neighbors, friends and co-workers for the gospel or if we are living so much for ourselves that Jesus is never seen in us. If we find ourselves in this category, Jesus says in **Revelation 3:18-22, "I advise you to buy from Me gold refined by fire so that you may become rich, and white garments so that you may clothe yourself, and that the shame of your nakedness will not be revealed; and eye salve to anoint your eyes so that you may see. 'Those whom I love, I reprove and discipline; therefore be zealous and repent. 'Behold, I stand at the door and knock; if anyone hears My voice and opens the door, I will come in to him and will dine with him, and he with Me. 'He who overcomes, I will grant to him to sit down with Me on My throne, as I also overcame and sat down with My Father on His throne. 'He who has an ear, let him hear what the Spirit says to the churches.'"**

He says to be zealous and repent. He wants us to stop being

self reliant and see life through His eyes. He wants us to truly surrender our lives to Him so we can point others to Him by our words and actions. Unlike Lot, people need to see our faith at work in our day to day lives so when we do speak of Christ, people will not laugh at us or think we are joking. Many people outside the church see Christians as hypocrites who do not live out what they say they believe and it is time we change that perception. If we are ever going to win this world for Christ, we can look at Lot's life and refuse to live like he did.

Dots to Connect

- Sin creeps into our lives slowly, and before we know it, we are where we should never be.

- We have a choice to stand up for our faith or go along with the crowd.

- We are called to be in the world but not of the world.

- How we act truly affects other people coming to Christ.

- We must surrender our lives to Christ so we can have an impact for Him.

- Jesus hates us living lukewarm Christian lives.

Chapter 11

Surrendering It All…

Genesis 21:1-5, "Then the Lord took note of Sarai as He had said, and the Lord did for Sarai as He had promised. So Sarai conceived and bore a son to Abraham in his old age, at the appointed time of which God had spoken to him. Abraham called the name of his son who was born to him, whom Sarai bore to him, Isaac. Then Abraham circumcised his son Isaac when he was eight days old, as God had commanded him. Now Abraham was one hundred years old when his son Isaac was born to him."

After years and years of waiting on God, Abraham and Sarah finally get the baby they have wanted for so long – what a day that must have been! All through their lives, God wanted to teach them what it truly meant to follow Him and trust Him. As we are coming to the end of this book, we want to do so with the most valuable lesson God wanted to teach Abraham and how for us, thousands of years later, He wants to teach us too. This is the dot we need to connect: **Everything is His.**

When we put this in perspective, this is what it means: our lives, our relationships, our spouses, and children are all His. Our homes, jobs, hobbies, talents and treasures are His also. Just like Abraham, He wants to know we recognize that fact. Sometimes that means He will test us to see if our hearts are really His. Do we care more for what He wants for us than what we want for ourselves? Are we willing to allow Him to move us to different places in our lives?

For Abraham, God wanted to know that even the long awaited son that was promised to him was not more important than his relationship with Him. So, He tested him to see where his heart was.

Genesis 22:1-3, Now it came about after these things, that God tested Abraham, and said to him, "Abraham!" And he said, "Here I am." He said, "Take now your son, your only son, whom you love, Isaac, and go to the land of Moriah, and offer him there as a burnt offering on one of the mountains of which I will tell you." So Abraham rose early in the morning and saddled his donkey, and took two of his young men with him and Isaac his son; and he split wood for the burnt offering, and arose and went to the place of which God had told him.

Offer him up as a burnt offering? Lay my beloved son down in order to kill him? Imagine what Abraham was thinking. The interesting part of this story is that Abraham just obeys God. He knows God has promised him Isaac and knows a nation will be built on his offspring so one way or another, God would come through. That is faith. That is years of seeing God show up in his life and that is where we need to be in our lives.

We have to learn to trust God no matter what He brings into our lives. Abraham could have fallen apart, took his son and ran the opposite direction or just plain refused to obey. Yet, his relationship with God was strong enough to withstand anything that was asked of him. Maybe you have lost your job or a loved one has passed away. Perhaps in this economy you have lost your home or your child has moved away. All of our lives we have to recognize that even behind change – there is God. If we are His children, He is always moving us to places where we can learn to trust Him more;

places where sometimes it is painful. Yet through it all, as we lay everything in our lives on the altar, God will get us to the place we can serve Him the best.

In his book "The Hole in our Gospel", Richard Stearns talks about how God moved him out of his successful business to becoming the President of World Vision:

Not sixty days earlier I had been CEO of Lenox, America's finest tableware company, producing and selling luxury goods to those who could afford them. I lived with my wife and five children in a ten-bedroom house on five acres just outside of Philadelphia. I drove a Jaguar to work every day, and my business travel took me to places such as Paris, Tokyo, London, and Florence. I flew first-class and stayed in the best hotels. I was respected in my community, attended a venerable suburban church, and sat on the board of my kids' Christian school. I was one of the good guys – you may say a "poster child" for the successful Christian life. I had never heard of Rakai,(Uganday) the place where my bubble would burst. But in just sixty days, God turned my life inside out and it would never be the same (Stearns, 2009).

God took Richard Stearns, a man who begged God to send someone else, and gave him a heart for those in need. He showed him what it truly meant to be a Christian and to give his life away. We live in a world where people are starving and children are dying and yet we live in our comfortable Christian circles without thinking of others around the world. For Richard, his heart was broken by the things that break God's heart and that is where God wants us all.

Just like Abraham, when God calls us to different places, He always provides exactly what we need. Just like the day Abraham was to offer up Isaac on the altar, sometimes God asks us to offer up the things that might be controlling our lives. For Richard Stearns, the struggle to leave the life he was perfectly happy with and do something he never wanted to do, was an incredible struggle and yet just like Abraham, when he came out on the other end, the blessings were more than he could imagine.

Many things in our lives can, and do, become more important than our relationship with God. There will always be that tension that sets our minds wondering: is this an idol to me? Do I flinch to the things of my flesh or do I flinch to the things of my faith? For Abraham, God tested him to see if his heart was truly His. Maybe God did this also for Abraham's sake – to allow Abraham to prove to himself that God really was the most important part of his life.

We see this in other parts of the bible where God tests people to see if their hearts are truly His.

Exodus 16:4, Then the Lord said to Moses, "Behold, I will rain bread from heaven for you; and the people shall go out and gather a day's portion every day, that I may test them, whether or not they will walk in My instruction."

Exodus 20:20, Moses said to the people, "Do not be afraid; for God has come in order to test you, and in order that the fear of Him may remain with you, so that you may not sin."

Deuteronomy 8:2, "You shall remember all the way which the Lord your God has led you in the wilderness these forty years, that He might humble you, testing you, to know what was in your heart, whether you would keep His commandments or not."

Deuteronomy 8:16, "In the wilderness He fed you manna which your fathers did not know, that He might humble you and that He might test you, to do good for you in the end."

Deuteronomy 13:3, "you shall not listen to the words of that prophet or that dreamer of dreams; for the Lord your God is testing you to find out if you love the Lord your God with all your heart and with all your soul."

2 Chronicles 32:31, "Even in the matter of the envoys of the rulers of Babylon, who sent to him to inquire of the wonder that had happened in the land, God left him alone only to test him, that He might know all that was in his heart."

We need to look at our lives and ask ourselves: do we view what God has given us as blessings from Him? Do we see Him behind all that happens to us?

Do we view our children as our possessions and do we take credit for the people they have turned out to be? Or, do we see the hand of God that has moved in their lives to be the kind of people they are today?

Do we see our business as successful because we are smart business people or do we give God all the credit for giving us the gifts and talents needed to be where we are today?

Do we look at our homes, our boats, our motorcycles or our R.V.'s and relish in the fact that we worked diligently to get them? Or, do we recognize the gift God gave us affording us the best schools and allowing us the best education which afforded us great jobs that provided us this lifestyle.

We have to connect the dot in our lives that everything we have has been given to us by God. Once we do – then we must learn to hold them loosely. If we think all things are ours – we tend to fall apart if they go away. Many times it takes difficult events in our lives to recognize the hand of God. So often, complicated situations and heartbreaks are what we need to show us and God, that we really do trust Him and we really do love Him. Sometimes we need to be reminded why we love God. Is it because He gives us what we want? Is it because He answers our prayers in the way we like? Sometimes when we get to complacent and put God to the side, we need to be reminded who really is in control.

For Abraham, God tells him to do something impossible and yet it seems that all through this event, he completely trusted God to keep his son safe.

Genesis 22:4-8, On the third day Abraham raised his eyes and saw the place from a distance. Abraham said to his young men, "Stay here with the donkey, and I and the lad will go over there; and we will worship and return to you."

Abraham seemed to know that God would not allow harm to come to Isaac. He was convinced that somehow they would both go and worship and then they would both return. That, we believe, is trust. He didn't know how or why God would bring them through this, but he had confidence that He would.

Therein lies the importance of spending time with God. The more we know someone, the easier it is to trust them. For us, as we watch the economy being shattered and people losing jobs and homes and money – we are learning that God promises to take care of us. That might not mean we will live in the lifestyle we have been accustomed to, but we have all the confidence in the world that He is with us.

Philippians 4:19 says, **"And my God will supply all your needs according to His riches in glory in Christ Jesus."** That is a promise.

When we are used to living a certain way, we expect it will always be the same. When we have always been able to go out to eat, go to the movies and vacation in the summer we assume it is God's job to make sure nothing ever changes. However, nowhere does the Bible ever promise that. The world is changing, the economy is changing and circumstances in life continually change. Life is filled with seasons.

Ecclesiastes 3:1-11, "There is an appointed time for everything. And there is a time for every event under heaven— A time to give

birth and a time to die; A time to plant and a time to uproot what is planted. A time to kill and a time to heal; A time to tear down and a time to build up. A time to weep and a time to laugh; A time to mourn and a time to dance. A time to throw stones and a time to gather stones; A time to embrace and a time to shun embracing. A time to search and a time to give up as lost; A time to keep and a time to throw away. A time to tear apart and a time to sew together; A time to be silent and a time to speak. A time to love and a time to hate; A time for war and a time for peace. What profit is there to the worker from that in which he toils? I have seen the task which God has given the sons of men with which to occupy themselves. He has made everything appropriate in its time. He has also set eternity in their heart, yet so that man will not find out the work which God has done from the beginning even to the end."

When we grasp that life is full of seasons, we can refuse to be devastated when things in our lives really do change.

Genesis 22:6, "Abraham took the wood of the burnt offering and laid it on Isaac his son, and he took in his hand the fire and the knife. So the two of them walked on together. Isaac spoke to Abraham his father and said, 'My father!' And he said, 'Here I am, my son.' And he said, 'Behold, the fire and the wood, but where is the lamb for the burnt offering?' Abraham said, 'God will provide for Himself the lamb for the burnt offering, my son.' So the two of them walked on together."

When Isaac questions his father about the lamb for the burnt offering, Abraham doesn't know how God will provide; He only knows that He will. This is a great lesson for all of us – resting in the fact that God will provide money for food or a place to sleep. He will make sure we get the job we need or the money for rent. Usually He waits until the last minute in order to show us exactly what He showed Abraham; He is always faithful.

Genesis 22:9-13, "Then they came to the place of which God had told him; and Abraham built the altar there and arranged the wood, and bound his son Isaac and laid him on the altar, on top of the wood. Abraham stretched out his hand and took the knife to slay his son. But the angel of the Lord called to him from heaven and said, 'Abraham, Abraham!' And he said, 'Here I am.' He said, 'Do not stretch out your hand against the lad, and do nothing to him; for now I know that you fear God, since you have not withheld your son, your only son, from Me.' Then Abraham raised his eyes and looked, and behold, behind him a ram caught in the thicket by his horns; and Abraham went and took the ram and offered him up for a burnt offering in the place of his son."

God came through and saved Isaac and Abraham came through by giving his most precious possession up to God. The test was performed and Abraham passed with flying colors. Looking back, twenty years earlier, Abraham probably would never have put Isaac on the altar because he didn't know God well enough to trust Him. When Isaac was finally born, Abraham was ready to give his all because he knew his God and he knew his God was faithful.

That is why we can rest assured knowing God's timing is always perfect. He has a plan for our lives and He moves in all our situations to get us where He can use us best. We have to learn that all through life there will be ups and downs and we need to be the constant straight line through it all. We need to have peace when we lose a job. We need to refuse to be fearful when the money is running low. That is the dot we need to connect – God is in the midst of all that happens to us and because of that fact alone, we can have peace.

The Blessings Of God • • •

We wanted to end this chapter by taking a quick look at the other side of this idea of Isaac possibly being Abraham's idol. For many of us, we have been taught to check our lives and make sure our children, sports, work, hobby or material possessions could possibly be more important to us than God. That is definitely something we should check in our lives but we want to take this a step further to take a look at the fact that God is the giver of the great blessings in our lives.

As we are writing the end of this book, we are in a cabin looking out over the most beautiful scenery. Out our window are large, beautiful pine trees and a spectacular blanket of pure, white snow covering the ground. We are able to look out to a pond that has small patches of water where ducks are swimming on and all we can do is thank God for the beauty He has created. He has allowed us to be here with our children and their spouses. He has given us wonderful things to see and to look at. We know these are gifts from Him to be enjoyed.

Gary Thomas in his book Pure Pleasure says this:

I grow weary of the teaching that, even for the redeemed, this good world that God created competes with Him instead of points me to Him. I tire of the thinking that separates pleasure from God; as if I'm supposed to "love" God more than I love engaging in a favorite pastime, such as running or enjoying a bite of chocolate. What a bizarre comparison! The fact is, I enjoy chocolate because God gave me taste buds, and any pleasure I derive from eating it is a pleasure designed and sustained by God. I can talk about enjoying running or eating chocolate as temptations toward idolatry, or I can talk about them as acts of worship that acknowledge and celebrate the God who makes physical exertion and the eating of chocolate both possible and enjoyable. "To the pure, all things are pure, but to those who are corrupted and do not believe, nothing is pure" Titus 1:15 (Thomas, 2009).

We need to be very careful to distinguish between the two. We can get so fearful that something God has given us as a blessing might be in competition with our love for Him. **Ecclesiastes 2:24 says: "There is nothing better for a man than to eat and drink**

and tell himself that his labor is good. This also I have seen that it is from the hand of God." If this is an issue for you, please pick up Gary Thomas' book "Pure Pleasure" and he can help you work through that issue. For Abraham, he recognized Isaac was his gift God had given him but he also trusted Him with his son. That is where we need to be – trusting God with the people and possessions that mean so much to us. He is trustworthy and we can learn this just like Abraham and Richard Stearns from World Vision did.

When we become a Christian, we give Jesus our lives; hands down. But life is a journey and along the way there are trials and tribulations that help us grow closer to Him. When we began looking at the life of Abraham, God called him from a pagan family and moved him to a distant land. He did not know how to trust God until he was forced into situations where he learned what that meant. For many people, God will use the loss of a job, an unwanted divorce, a wayward child, or depressed economy to force us to stop trusting ourselves. He wants us to get to the place, just like Abraham that we, hands down, say: "God, everything I have is yours and I trust that whatever you do with them is Your perfect will for me."

This is the dot we want to connect…and this is how the Christian life works.

"God, everything I have is yours and I trust that whatever you do with them is Your perfect will for me."

Dots to Connect

- We need to learn that everything came from and belongs to God.

- When we surrender our lives to Christ we recognize our lives, relationships, spouses, families, children, jobs, hobbies, talents, and treasures are all His.

- Sometimes He will test us to see if we care more for Him or more for ourselves.

- We must learn to trust God no matter what He brings into our lives.

- We must have a strong relationship with God in order to be able to withstand anything that comes into our lives.

- Everything in our lives have been given to us by God and we must hold them loosely.

- The more time we spend with God, getting to know Him, the easier it is to trust Him with everything in our lives.

- Life will be constantly changing and we need to learn how to deal with change as part of God's plan for our lives.

- God gives us wonderful blessings in our lives and we need to make sure and recognize His hand in all that we have.

Chapter 12

The Simplicity of a Verse

P*salm 119:24 "Your testimonies also are my delight; They are my counselors."*

As we come to the end of this book - we want to recognize that we have something Abraham and Sarai never had – His written Word. So often in life we just need to be encouraged. Sometimes we just want to know that things are going to be okay and usually that comes in the form of a friend. But, many times, our heart's desire is to hear from God, to hear Him speak to us telling us He is still there, He is still on the throne and He hasn't forgotten us. Abraham and Sarai went years and years without contact from God and yet we differ from them because we have God's Word. We have the ability to look back and see how God works, how He answered prayers, and how He weaved His plan throughout the lives of those in the Bible.

As Christians, the Bible has to be held in high regard. Doctrine is important. Knowing the context and the interpretation is important. But sometimes, we don't want a long sermon. Many times we don't want to know what the Greek or the Hebrew in the original language means. We just want a simple verse that will help us make it through the day. A verse. Sometimes that is all we need to make it through the difficult days we are going through.

Our Bibles can be used as a journal to see how God has answered prayers. For me (Rob), writing in my Bible is something I do to help remember something. It is so easy to forget the things God has done, so when a verse touches my life, I write the situation next to the verse. I am planning on leaving my Bible as a legacy for our children so they can see the struggles I have gone through and yet how the simplicity of a verse gave me hope and peace. I want our children to see how God's Word impacted my days on earth.

For this last chapter, we decided to go through my Bible and write out some of the situations I was going through and how certain verses touched my life. One thing I have learned is to sit and ponder a verse. We can get so wrapped up in trying to read a number of chapters in a day and yet many times we end up reading our Bible just to cross this item off our list of "to do's" for the day. Instead, I have learned to take it slow. If a verse seems to speak to me, I will sit and think about it; sometimes I will ponder on it for a couple days. I will spend the time to cross reference the verse so I can read other verses regarding the same subject. That is when I learn the most; when I take a verse and let God use it to impact my life.

Hopefully, you will see how reading our Bible truly can affect our attitudes regarding the issues we are faced with daily. Here are some situations in our lives where God used His Word to speak to us.

Proverbs 2:1-10, "My son, if you will receive my words and treasure my commandments within you, make your ear attentive to wisdom, incline your heart to understanding; for if you cry for discernment, lift your voice for understanding; if you seek her as silver and search for her as for hidden treasures; then you will discern the fear of the Lord and discover the knowledge of God. For the Lord gives wisdom; from His mouth comes knowledge and understanding. He stores up sound wisdom for the upright; He is a shield to those who walk in integrity, guarding the paths of justice, and He preserves the way of His godly ones. Then you will discern righteousness and justice and equity and every good

course. For wisdom will enter your heart and knowledge will be pleasant to your soul." As I was reading this, I realized how important it is to read my Bible on a daily basis. I can't just wake up one morning and know God and His ways and what He has in store for my life. To receive His words, I need to read His words. This will always take some effort on my part. This verse made me recognize that in order to have the wisdom needed to run my business or deal with my wife or children in a Godly manner – I need to be seeking Him. He is the One who will give me the wisdom I need in life; but my part is reading, treasuring, seeking, keeping my ears attentive and inclining my heart toward understanding. Our minds need to be renewed on a daily basis and since **Hebrews 4:12** says, **"For the word of God is living and active and sharper than any two-edged sword, and piercing as far as the division of soul and spirit, of both joints and marrow, and able to judge the thoughts and intentions of the heart"**, then I need to recognize His word is living and active and He will speak to me at different times. Sometimes I read a verse and I have no need for it at the moment but a year later I can read the same verse and it is just what I need for that day.

Colossians 3:2, "Set your mind on the things above, not on the things that are on earth." There are many days when the tragedies of life can get to me. One day in particular, many things were going on in our business and it seemed overwhelming...bordering on hopelessness. As I was reading the next morning I came across this verse. I sat and thought about what God was trying to teach me, I realized that my mind can get so focused on the things of this earth and yet, God wants me to keep my mind on eternal things. I need to keep my focus on God's plans for me, which many times can involve difficult situations, since it is in those times I learn to trust Him. We can get so absorbed in our problems, without ever looking at them as a way to grow closer to God, keeping in mind He wants us to trust Him for things instead of trusting ourselves.

Philippians 4:5, "Let your gentle spirit be known to all men. The Lord is near." This particular day, I was saddened by how someone had been treating me. My first response was to lash out at this person and make sure they understood my side of the story. As I read this verse, I realized that God was calling me to have a gentle spirit and treat all others with gentleness; even the person who was upsetting me. I learned that being gentle meant I needed to have patience without retaliating regardless if I am being mistreated. As I prayed each day, God changed my heart and took away the anger I had been feeling. He gave me the ability to be gentle in the circumstance.

Proverbs 3:5-6, "Trust in the Lord with all your heart and do not lean on your own understanding. In all your ways acknowledge Him, and He will make your paths straight." In my Bible I have four different events, from my life, written by this verse. Sometimes I need to make sure I am trusting in the Lord and not trusting in myself. By keeping this verse in front of me, I always want to make sure He is guiding my paths day by day.

Proverbs 8:34-35, "Blessed is the man who listens to me, watching daily at my gates, waiting at my doorposts. For he who finds Me finds life and obtains favor from the Lord." This verse is a reminder that seeking God and His wisdom has to be a daily occurrence.

Proverbs 16:1, "The plans of the heart belong to man, but the answer of the tongue is from the Lord." This verse was instrumental for me as I was walking into a meeting regarding a light bulb we had invested in. Our plan was that this light bulb would benefit the lighting industry and we were in this meeting to show these clients our product. This was a great reminder to me that I could give this presentation but it would be God who would give us the outcome He wanted for us.

Proverbs 16:7, "When a man's ways are pleasing to the Lord, He makes even his enemies to be at peace with him."

Proverbs 17:14, "The beginning of strife is like letting out water,

So abandon the quarrel before it breaks out.'

Proverbs 22:1, "A good name is to be more desired than great wealth, Favor is better than silver and gold." These three verses helped me through a business deal where I felt like I was being charged more than the original bid. I was frustrated with the man who I had given the work to and so I told him I did not feel what he was charging our company was fair and I refused to pay it. When I read Proverbs 16:7, the first day, it was like the Lord was telling me that if I would do what pleased Him, He would give me peace with this man I was dealing with. The second day, I came upon Proverbs 17:14 and I felt like I needed to partially give in to this man in order to stop contention before it started; so I called and told him I would pay him half of what he was asking. A couple days later, I was reading Proverbs 22:1, and I realized that my name as a Christian was more valuable than any amount of money. I wanted to be known as a man who loved God and someone who had integrity and yet I knew if desiring wealth was more important – my reputation as a Christian would be harmed. I called him and told him I would pay the entire bill because I knew God would bless my decision to be honoring to Him. For me, this situation was a reminder how God uses His Word when He wants to speak into my life.

Proverbs 21:1, "The heart is like channels of water in the hand of the Lord; He turns it wherever He wishes."

Proverbs 21:31, "The horse is prepared for the day of battle, But victory belongs to the Lord." These two verses have been instrumental in my life on a daily basis. I have come to recognize that God turns people's hearts wherever He wants; to get me to the place He wants for me. We have land for sale, that we need to sell; yet we have learned that when God's timing is perfect, He will move on someone's heart to buy it. We have a man we wanted to hire and we were assured by these verses that God would move on this man's heart to come to work for us if that was His will. In my Bible beside Proverbs 21:31, I have written down many situations where we have been totally prepared for meetings we were going into; yet all the while knowing, God would get credit for any victory in our business dealings.

Proverbs 22:26, "Do not be among those who give pledges, among those who become guarantors for debts." We have a development business and were getting ready to build a spec house. The loan had been approved and the documents were ready to be signed at the bank. Before I signed the papers, I went on a fishing trip, was gone a week, upon return attended a Bible study where the pastor was talking about this very verse. He was cautioning people to make sure before borrowing any money that they were not over leveraging. I started feeling uncomfortable about our decision to borrow this money and I called our banker the next day and called off the loan and decided not to build the spec home. One year later, I was told by people at this bank that I had made a smart decision to not borrow the money the year before since the economy had taken a turn for the worse. I knew, once again, that God's Word had saved us.

Proverbs 28:19, "He who tills his land will have plenty of food, but he who follows empty pursuits will have poverty in plenty." This verse is a constant reminder to work diligently in our business.

Genesis 39:2, "The Lord was with Joseph, so he became a successful man. And he was in the house of his master, the Egyptian."

Genesis 39:21, "But the Lord was with Joseph and extended kindness to him, and gave him favor in the sight of the chief jailer."

Genesis 39:23, "The chief jailer did not supervise anything under Joseph's charge because the Lord was with him; and whatever he did, the Lord made to prosper." Last Christmas I was frustrated with the economy, our business wasn't doing very well and I felt as though God wasn't that interested in my life. As I read these verses, it dawned on me that for all Joseph went through; slavery, being unjustly accused, sold by his brothers, and taken to a foreign country at a young age... all of this probably made Joseph feel like God had abandoned him also. Yet, we can see from these verses – God was with Joseph even though he most likely didn't feel like it. Reading these verses reminded me that God was right there through all my problems and I could trust Him to get me where He wanted me just like He did with Joseph.

As we have been going through financial difficulties, we sometimes feel God has forgotten us and yet **Ecclesiastes 7:14** says, **"In the day of prosperity be happy, but in the day of adversity consider— God has made the one as well as the other so that man will not discover anything that will be after him."** We are learning that God hasn't disappeared during the days of adversity – we are recognizing He is in control of both!

Proverbs 30:8-9, "Keep deception and lies far from me, give me neither poverty nor riches; feed me with the food that is my portion, that I not be full and deny You and say, 'Who is the Lord?' Or that I not be in want and steal, and profane the name of my God." For me (Lisa), God is teaching me how to be content with what God is giving us. I am recognizing that when we have prosperity, it is easy to forget God and to trust ourselves. I find it easy to trust God when there is money in the bank, but when that is gone, I have learned what it means to truly trust God and His provision for us. This has built trust in my life for Him and I am learning that He alone provides for our needs.

1 Chronicles 28:9, "As for you, my son Solomon, know the God of your father, and serve Him with a whole heart and a willing mind; for the Lord searches all hearts, and understands every intent of the thoughts. If you seek Him, He will let you find Him; but if you forsake Him, He will reject you forever." We have a friend who is not certain he is a Christian but he is seeking God and wanting to know the truth. As I was reading this verse, it helped me pray for our friend since God promises that if someone is seeking Him, He will let them find Him.

These are some of our experiences that hopefully you will see how Scripture can be used in our daily lives. We thought it would be helpful to write out some additional verses that might be an encouragement in your life. We are all struggling through life regardless if it is an illness, a loss of job, a failing marriage or a sinful past. God wants us to be reminded that He is here, with us, and He hasn't forgotten us and sometimes He uses just one simple verse to do so!

The Battle is God's!
2 Chronicles 20:15, "and he said, 'Listen, all Judah and the inhabitants of Jerusalem and King Jehoshaphat, thus says the Lord to you, 'Do not fear or be dismayed because of this great multitude, for the battle is not yours but God's.'"

Stand and see what God will do!
2 Chronicles 20:17, "'You need not fight in this battle; station yourselves, stand and see the salvation of the Lord on your behalf, O Judah and Jerusalem.' Do not fear or be dismayed; tomorrow go out to face them, for the Lord is with you."

God does not forsake us!
Nehemiah 9:17, "They refused to listen, and did not remember Your wondrous deeds which You had performed among them; so they became stubborn and appointed a leader to return to their slavery in Egypt. But You are a God of forgiveness, Gracious and compassionate, Slow to anger and abounding in lovingkindness; And You did not forsake them."

Everything is His – so why do we worry?
Nehemiah 9:6, "You alone are the Lord. You have made the heavens, the heaven of heavens with all their host, The earth and all that is on it, the seas and all that is in them. You give life to all

of them and the heavenly host bows down before You."

God always knows when we are sad and grieved
Psalm 6:6-7, "I am weary with my sighing; Every night I make my bed swim, I dissolve my couch with my tears. My eye has wasted away with grief; It has become old because of all my adversaries."

We eagerly watch for God's answer
Psalm 5:1-3, "Give ear to my words, O Lord, Consider my groaning. Heed the sound of my cry for help, my King and my God, for to You I pray. In the morning, O Lord, You will hear my voice; in the morning I will order my prayer to You and eagerly watch."

We can sleep in peace at night
Psalm 4:8, "In peace I will both lie down and sleep, For You alone, O Lord, make me to dwell in safety."

Sometimes God seems distant and yet that doesn't mean He is not there
Psalm 10:1, "Why do You stand afar off, O Lord? Why do You hide Yourself in times of trouble?"

We can have confidence God will answer our prayers
Psalm 17:6, "I have called upon You, for You will answer me, O God; incline Your ear to me, hear my speech."

God delights in us
Psalm 18:19, "He brought me forth also into a broad place; He rescued me, because He delighted in me."

We never have cause to be envious of those who are evil but successful
Psalm 37:1-2, "Do not fret because of evildoers, be not envious toward wrongdoers. For they will wither quickly like the grass

and fade like the green herb."

God establishes our steps
Psalm 37:23-24, "The steps of a man are established by the Lord, and He delights in his way. When he falls, he will not be hurled headlong, because the Lord is the One who holds his hand."

The Lord laughs at the wicked
Psalm 37:12-13, "The wicked plots against the righteous and gnashes at him with his teeth. The Lord laughs at him, for He sees his day is coming."

We don't need to take life so serious since we know our days are numbered!
Psalm 39:4-5, "Lord, make me to know my end And what is the extent of my days; Let me know how transient I am. Behold, You have made my days as handbreadths, And my lifetime as nothing in Your sight; Surely every man at his best is a mere breath."

We never have to fear regardless of the change in our circumstances
Psalm 46:1-3, "God is our refuge and strength, a very present help in trouble. Therefore we will not fear, though the earth should change and though the mountains slip into the heart of the sea; though its waters roar and foam, though the mountains quake at its swelling pride."

He knows everything and everything is His – even us!
Psalm 50:10-11, "For every beast of the forest is Mine, the cattle on a thousand hills. I know every bird of the mountains, and everything that moves in the field is Mine."

Even when our faith seems joyless, God will restore this to us
Psalm 51:12, "Restore to me the joy of Your salvation And sustain me with a willing spirit."

<u>**God can call down angels to help us if need be!**</u>
Matthew 26:52-53, "Then Jesus said to him, 'Put your sword back into its place; for all those who take up the sword shall perish by the sword. Or do you think that I cannot appeal to My Father, and He will at once put at My disposal more than twelve legions of angels?'"

This is where we need to get our encouragement, for in the Bible are the Words of God to us. He wants us to know He loves us, cares for us and forgives us. He wants us to remember He is always in control and even though He seems silent, He is still working behind the scenes in our lives. He wants us to keep in mind that He is awesome and powerful and can change people, change hearts and change situations to get us to the places He wants us.

This is the God we love and serve and many times, when He seems silent, it gives us great opportunities to read about others who have been there before us. As we see the great men and women of the Bible struggle with the same things we do; fear, anxiety, discouragement, and the silence of God, we begin to have hope. As we read His Word, we can relax as His Words begin to encourage us and calm our hearts as we grow to know Him better. The more we can see God for who He really is – the more peaceful our lives become.

Connecting the Dots between our life and our faith.

That must be the goal of our lives. Our daily lives and our faith in Christ must not be two separate parts but must be interwoven on a daily basis. Our hope and prayer is that Abraham has given us a glimpse of what that should look like in our own lives.

Dots to Connect

- We need to be encouraged by God's Word on a daily basis.

- Sometimes we just need a verse that will help us through the day.

- Reading our Bibles will affect our attitudes as we face difficult situations.

- We can have hope, for what we are going through, as we see men and women in the Bible who struggled through the same things we do.

- Our daily lives and our daily faith must be connected in order to affect this world for Jesus.

References

http://www.keepbelieving.com

Stearns, Richard (2009). *The Hole in Our Gospel.* Nashville, TN: Thomas Nelson, Inc.

Thomas, Gary (2009). Pure Pleasure: *Why do Christians Feel so Bad for Feeling Good?* Grand Rapids, MI: Zondervan.

Connecting the Dots Between Life and Faith

If you have any questions or comments, please e-mail us at:

lisalaizure@aol.com
or
robslaizure@aol.com

Visit us at our website
www.dollarchristianbooks.com